Diary of Our Miracle Child

The Journey With Our Daughter's Lymphatic Malformation

By: Eliezer & Tzirel Miller

Endorsements

The "Diary of Our Miracle Child" highlights an amazing journey of struggle and perseverance, of pain and love and an unwavering trust that Hashem is the guiding source for all that we go through and that it's always good. Eliezer and Tzirel's challenges are beautifully detailed with each moment heroically endured and lovingly traveled.

- Dr. Feigie Russ, Psy.D

I have known the Miller family for many years, and to say that their journey was anything short of miraculous would be an untruth to the highest degree.

This book has a single thread that weaves itself through the fabric of every page of every chapter. That is the power of Emunah. The rock-solid faith that a young couple can exude in the face of such trying and challenging circumstances is beyond belief.

This story is not just a tale of birth and renewal but rather one of courage, trust, and dependency on a force greater than us all. As you get to know the Miller family, be prepared to laugh and cry with them as they embrace each new step on their trajectory towards becoming bigger, better, and stronger parents.

Most of all, get ready to be inspired - inspired by what being connected to G-d really means. For anyone who has ever spent time in a delivery room will tell you that there is no greater revelation of His omnipotent presence than when an untainted soul enters this world, all the more so when it is a special soul.

- R' Heshy Kahan

Table of Contents

Dedication

Refuah Shelaima for: Shalva Nechama Bas Tzirel
For a complete cure and Recovery for: Shalva Nechama Bas Tzirel

Authors forward

We never dreamt of writing a book, so the thought never came across our minds for us to write. Being that we had a unique miraculous journey with our daughter, starting from pregnancy with her up until this very point of Shalva's life, people have mentioned it would be a great story to share. Hearing that over and over again did not talk to us, as neither of us were authors nor do we have a passion to write.

In general, we keep our lives to ourselves and don't like to publicize our personal lives. We like when things are kept low key and quiet, therefore we did not want to share our journey of Shalva's life.

Through a life coaching course, I built up my courage and decided I can write. I spoke it over with my husband and he agreed that it can be a great opportunity. We discussed this more, we decided if our journey of our precious princess's life can help, inspire, encourage, or help anyone get closer to G-D it would be very worthwhile to write a book.

Once we made our decision, we started right away, and began writing the very next day. Writing a book takes a lot of effort and time, so it's a good thing we started before knowing how much it would actually entail. Once we jumped into it, we knew were going to do it all the way, there was no backing out.

We spent hours together writing this book, as a team, to give it all we've got. Our goal of this book was to uplift and inspire others, so we made sure to put our heart and soul into it, from beginning until its completion. Being a full-time mother and wife, which is a full-time job in and of itself, and with a little baby, there was no way for me to just set a specific time to write. I took every quiet moment, whether it was while I was feeding the baby, waiting for my kids to get home from school, or a spare minute in the day. My husband works full time and spends his non-working time learning. He still made an effort to spend every available minute to write along with me. Because we wanted to work on this at every free moment, we drafted the book on my phone!

We really hope and pray that this book will reach all those that need to hear this message!

The only way to write this book was with complete teamwork and unity of us working together. We want to thank Hashem for giving us such an opportunity, for continuously helping us every step of the way, and for everything!

We thank our dear parents, grandparents, family, and friends, for all the continuous, support, help, and most of all for the endless prayers.

Thank you to our Rabbi's that guided us every step of the way and made themselves available to give us chizuk, strength, and the courage we needed to get through it all.

Thank you to all the teams of doctors, nurses, and surgeons for giving and continuing to give Shalva all the health care you can possibly give. Thank you for all the time spent explaining everything from her diagnosis to her procedures, and everything in between.

We want to take a moment to thank Chai Lifeline for all the support, volunteers, food, and help that they provided for us. We could not have done it without them. They always extended themselves above and beyond what would be imagined.

We would like to thank our neighbors, community, and chessed organizations for all the help, support, and delicious meals that were sent over during the trying times.

Thank you, Yael Rosenblum, for constantly being there for us any time we called, and always with a smile. We're so humbled by the amount of times you saved the day in times of dire need. You became such a big part of our family, and we are forever grateful. We would also like to thank you for your expert editing at a rapid pace. Your devotion and dedication have been instrumental in shaping this book. You did an amazing job!

Thank you to our wonderful publishing and editing team for all the time that was spent having this book put together.

This journey was not an easy one, through all the love, support, and help we received, we persevered and were able to continue on. We really got to feel and experience the truth of Mi K'amcha Yisrael (Who is like the Jewish nation).

CHAPTER: 1

It was February 2019, and the anomaly scan was coming up on Monday. Up until this point of the pregnancy, everything seemed to be healthy, regular, and normal. There were no alarms or concerns as the blood work, sonogram, and checkups were perfect.

It was Friday, and I was getting my last-minute preparations ready for Shabbos (Shabbat). It was about fifteen minutes before candle lighting time (A customary tradition to Light candles to honor and welcome in the Shabbat) as I had a scary, intense thought that popped into my head that I couldn't stop thinking about. I had some sort of feeling that there was a complication or concern with the pregnancy. I quickly checked my lab result from the latest blood work and reassured myself that everything was alright. I felt very confused as I don't generally obsess, and I don't fantasize about negative, scary things. This frightened me, though I told myself everything was okay. It must be my pregnancy hormones messing with my mind and thoughts. I mentioned this to my husband, and he wasn't concerned.

Over the weekend, that thought kept popping into my head. On one hand, I felt it was a mother's instinct. On the other hand, I just tried pushing that thought away and kept telling myself everything is and will be okay. I'll get my reassurance on Monday at my anomaly scan.

Monday came, and the plan was that I'd drop my toddler off at my mother's work, and she'd watch him for up to two hours. Then I'd take a taxi to the clinic for my anomaly scan. Thinking of saving a few dollars, I had my husband take me and stay along, which was such Hashgachas Pratis (Divine Providence).

Being that he was working, I met him near his job site, and we drove twenty-five minutes to the clinic in his work van, which was a bumpy ride. Little did we know it was the start of the bumpiest journey in our lives.

The appointment was at 10:30 a.m. The sonographer did the exam, and when I asked about the results, she told me to wait in the room for the doctor. A few minutes later, the sonographer came back to the exam room, handed me the phone and told me the Doctor wanted to speak with me. I felt a major chill down my spine.

I picked up the phone, and on the other side of the line, I was introduced to an MFM (Maternal Fetal Medicine Doctor), who sounded seriously concerned and asked who I was with. When I told her I was here with my husband, she said she wanted me to come to see her in the hospital immediately without any further details.

My heart was pounding and felt crushed, as I thought of the worst-case scenario. In tears, we immediately rushed out of the clinic and ran to the hospital. When we got there, we were told that the doctor was on her lunch break, and we should be back in an hour. In the meantime, we went to the Bikur Cholim room (Kosher Pantry). As we were heading out, we spotted my ob-gyn.

With his true sympathy, empathy, and positivity, he told us what he heard. It seems like the baby had an organ growing externally, and it'll need one or two surgeries after birth. Other than that, everything seemed to be fine and healthy. We should just daven (pray), and there was nothing to be worried about!

What a relief! We felt so grateful and were able to breathe again. We headed back up to meet the MFM, where we were told to go to the exam room and have their sonographer redo the entire anomaly exam. When I asked if everything was okay, I was told to wait for the doctor.

A few minutes later, the MFM came in herself and retook the images. At this point, I knew something was definitely not right! As she was nearing the end I asked if everything was okay, to which she responded, you wouldn't be here if everything was okay, with no further details.

The exam was over, and we were told to wait in the waiting room to speak with the MFM in her office. In the meantime, I went into the hallway and saw my ob-gyn again. I updated him and inquired what he had heard. He said they didn't want to tell him anything until they spoke with me first, as they want to be the ones to tell me what's going on. He reassured me that he'll come back soon to see what was happening.

I went back to the waiting area and told my husband about the talk with the ob-gyn. Now, feeling and thinking the worst, I was very emotional and saying Tehillim (Psalms).

CHAPTER: 2

My husband then went for a little walk in the hallway. He looked out the window and started staring at the skyline of Manhattan, he was just taking everything in. At that very moment, he knew his life was about to change forever. He had a shiver down his spine.

As we were scared and anxiously waiting, every minute felt like an hour. Finally, after a long forty-five minutes of waiting, we were called into the MFM's office. She had us both take a seat and offered us a cup of water. We knew with her tone of voice and the look on her face that the news was no good.

She apologized for the long wait and explained that what appeared on the images she'd never seen and had to forward all the images to other doctors in Manhattan. They had to explain the situation for her to understand it and give it over.

She closed the lights and started going through the images with us and started explaining the diagnosis to us. It's very rare, less than 5% worldwide. From the 5%, less than 1% of people have the diagnosis in the area this fetus has it in, and scientists are still studying this. With that being the case, she had very little knowledge about this diagnosis and didn't have answers to our questions.

With that being said, they recommended, encouraged, and tried to persuade us to have a medical abortion. Being that we are religious orthodox Jews, she knew to advise us to speak to our Rabbi. She then continued by saying no one has to know, no one will judge you, and you won't have to deal with this unknown, scary diagnosis.

Immediately I burst into tears and said I'd never have an abortion, no matter what. God is in control, and I will let Him run the show. It wasn't even a question, I felt there was absolutely no need to ask a Rabbi. I was sure and confident with my decision to keep the pregnancy alive!

She went on to say that if you choose not to terminate the pregnancy, it'll most likely be a miscarriage, possibly even later on in the pregnancy, or a stillbirth, or have a very low chance of survival. If it does make it past birth, they don't know if the baby will make it past a few hours, a few days, weeks, months or years. She wouldn't accept a straight-out no and advised us to think about it and get spiritual guidance.

As we were shedding tears, there was a knock on the door. Our ob-gyn walked in. My husband asked him for some words of encouragement, not knowing the verdict of what was happening. He said to remember Hashem (G-D) is in control. Just rely on Hashem (G-D) and Daven (Pray), and everything will be good. And with that, he gave my husband a big hug.

The MFM briefly updated him with the information she just told us and then continued on to say she doesn't have much information, though it's very crucial and important for them to do a genetic amniocentesis (which tests the amniotic fluids in the womb and tests the DNA from the cells for health conditions and diagnosis).

The ob-gyn said if that's what the MFM needs us to do, we shouldn't hesitate, and should go along with doing this procedure. This is part of us doing our hishtadlus (personal effort). So, we agreed to it.

They had their staff stay late for every moment was crucial. They didn't want to waste any time, and they wanted to get as much information as possible gathered up as soon as they could to continue further their own research.

As I signed the consent form and read that the amniocentesis procedure had a risk of a miscarriage, I broke down in uncontrollable tears. I knew the only power I had was in my tefillos (prayers), so I cried and cried whilst I davened (prayed). My husband was very calming and tried reassuring me that it's all in Hashem's hands, and just keep davening (praying), and it will all be good!

After a long wait, they called us into the room and said we will poke a needle by your abdomen wall, and it should take about twenty seconds. I shouldn't talk or move because a little bit of a move can cause the needle to go in the wrong place which can cause a miscarriage.

I was holding back my tears. As emotional as I felt, as scared as I was, I didn't want to move. I just took those moments to say some more Tehillim (Psalms), poured out my heart and spoke to Hashem (G-D) in my mind and in my own words.

My husband, being supportive, holding my hand, tried to give me words of encouragement when the doctor said no talking and no moving as they frightened us again, saying any movement I made could be the cause of a miscarriage.

The procedure was not working out in the time frame of twenty seconds. They were caught up in difficulty and couldn't seem to spot the amniotic fluid. It took them three pokes in different areas of my abdomen, and about twenty minutes later, until the amniocentesis was completed. For all those who don't know what the amniocentesis procedure is, it's a long, thin needle inserted in the abdominal wall. The physical and emotional pain was way beyond what words can possibly describe. The doctor's bedside manner was very poor, with a major attitude surrounded with lots of negativity.

CHAPTER: 3

It was 7:30 p.m., and we finally arrived back home. Our 4 kids at the time were eagerly waiting for us as they didn't have a clue as to what was going on. My mother watched our 18 months old from the morning, and the rest of the children as they got home from school. I walked in the door and my kids came running, excited to see us. I couldn't stop bawling and crying that I was so grateful for these four beautifully healthy children and kept Thanking Hashem (G-D).

After a few minutes, my mother called me aside as she was worried, nervous, concerned, and scared since all day when she tried reaching out to me. I told her I couldn't talk now, just daven (pray) that everything would be okay. She had lots of questions, and I just couldn't talk. I was so emotional I burst into uncontrollable tears. I thanked my mother for all her help and told her I'd be in touch with her tomorrow when I calmed down a bit.

The day was long and overwhelming, and my husband was strong and emotionally supportive with all the news coming in. At the moment he handled it in a very healthy way. However, when we got home, reality hit him, and he didn't know how to handle his emotions. He started to shut down and drift off. He preoccupied himself with all sorts of outlets. He worked more hours and did anything to try to run and avoid reality.

I was in shambles, torn, and felt crushed into pieces. For one thing, I heard awful news about my pregnancy and my world was falling apart. My husband was out to lunch, and my children needed me to be sane, healthy, and happy. And I felt I was going through all this alone!

Throughout my life, I kept my personal experiences on the quieter end of things, especially with such news. I did not want to be the talk of the town and wanted to keep it on the quieter side. Also, there is a tradition in our Jewish culture that blessings come when things are kept quiet and on the low. So, I didn't want to share any of this with people.

The next day, the ob-gyn called me to see how I was feeling and how we were holding up and doing emotionally. He gave me some chizuk (inspiration) and reminded me that Hashem is in control, listen to the doctors as that's your hishtadlus, (personal effort) and just Daven to Hashem. He is the ultimate Rofeh (Healer).

He told me that this pregnancy is high risk and that I will have to switch to using the MFM team. He reassured me that if I have any questions or concerns, I can always reach out to him. He asked me to keep him updated and he was trying to do some research regarding this diagnosis.

He delivered my four children that I had up until this point, and I really wanted him to deliver me this time as well. He said he could try getting permission from the hospital, and if not, he would come to the delivery to be an advocate for me. That was very reassuring to me.

We had very frequent appointments as they wanted to monitor the situation very carefully. They didn't allow toddlers or children to come to any of the appointments, which made it more difficult. So, we told my parents and a few siblings that we needed help with the children. At the time we had four children under the age of seven.

I always liked to be there for friends and family and didn't like taking favors from others. Being that no children were allowed to come, and I needed my husband to be with me, we had no choice but to ask for and accept favors. It's such a blessing to be on the giving end, and I really learned to appreciate that when I constantly need help from others.

My toddler was very attached to me as I was a stay-at-home mom. He had never been apart from me during his waking hours, so this was very hard on him. He did not take to this situation well. I would drop him off at a family member and give him lots of hugs and kisses. I tried talking to him and telling him I'll be back soon and that I'm just going for an appointment. Being that he was so young, he didn't understand. When I was leaving, we tried offering him treats, toys, and all different things, but all he wanted was his Mommy. As heartbroken as I was, I had no choice but to go. Leaving your toddler crying is an awful feeling; he would not give up on crying. He would run near the door and cry on the floor until he fell asleep. I thought and hoped that with time, he'd get used to it and accept it, but that never happened. His response was like this until the end of the pregnancy.

CHAPTER: 4

Leaving my toddler crying and going to appointments with my husband, who was not taking this news well, was very difficult. He was in fight or flight mode. Being that he was physically present, he would drive me back and forth and stay with me, but he was not able to give me the emotional support that I needed. I felt I was suffering in silence.

This added lots of heat and tension between us. He did his part and took me to all my appointments and therefore missed out on lots of work. We would ask the MFM doctor lots of questions each visit, and we just kept getting lots of negative feedback. The MFM strongly felt we should terminate the pregnancy, and she would ask me at least three or four times each appointment, are you sure you don't want to terminate? You have a couple more weeks for you to medically abort. You don't want to regret it, etc. She felt very strongly and was very passionate about aborting! I kept telling her I didn't want to abort, I would never abort, and please stop asking me.

Being that there's not much information about this diagnosis, she must've wanted to protect herself. She told us the chances the baby will make it are very slim. However, if it makes it, it'll possibly not be able to use the bathroom, not be able to eat, walk, talk, or breathe on its own. It may be hospital bound or wheelchair bound. She prepared us for the worst nightmare.

I would come home without any appetite and couldn't sleep. I tried to hold back my tears and be there for my children. There were times I would burst out into tears in front of them, and they would ask me why I was crying and what happened. I didn't want to cause them any distress or anxiety, so I would just say I'm thinking of some very sad things that someone told me.

I heard the song from Waterbury Mesivta, "Tatty My King." I internalized those words, and I would listen to them over and over again. I poured out my heart to Hashem, crying uncontrollably and as those words penetrated my heart, I would cry and sing along. I was very emotionally attached to this song, and it brought me very close to Hashem (G-D). When I was done, I just breathed a bit, and I felt Hashem's presence. I felt Him holding my hand tight!

I had a hard time opening a siddur (prayer book) to daven (pray), though I was constantly talking and crying out to Hashem in my own words. I was saying Tehillim (Psalms), and I tried to be careful with saying the Bracha of Asher Yatzar (Blessing that is said after using the bathroom) with extra kavana (concentration).

As every appointment came up, I dreaded going to them more and more. They would do each sonogram and measure. They would show me the images, tell me the size, and continue to be more pessimistic about the diagnosis. They constantly tried to pressure us and gave us more and more reasons to try convincing us to terminate the pregnancy.

They kept telling us the clock was ticking and soon it would be too late to terminate, and I asked the MFM to please respect us. We do not want to terminate this pregnancy. I'm going to have this baby unless G-D wants otherwise. I asked the MFM to please stop bringing up abortion, as that was crushing my heart emotionally. However, she did not respect my request. It seemed she was eager and excited to have this baby aborted.

After one appointment with the MFM, she was just being so rude with her attitude and tried to persuade us again into abortion. I came home and broke down. I couldn't handle these emotions. I called my ob-gyn and told him what was going on and how poorly I was being treated. He apologized and felt really bad about that and said he would call the MFM on my behalf.

I was really appreciative that he was so on board with this pregnancy, and I felt he really genuinely cared. Having a doctor with compassion, empathy, and good bedside manners made a world of difference.

The next day, I got a call, and when I heard the voice of the MFM on the other end of the line, my heart started pounding. She said I'm calling to inform you that I was in touch with your ob-gyn, and he told me that you're going through a difficult time emotionally and that you don't want me to bring up abortion any longer. She apologized and said, from now on, she won't bring it up! I thanked her for her understanding, and I davened (prayed) that she would actually keep to her word.

After that phone call, I called my ob-gyn to thank him for advocating and sticking up on my behalf. He told me had he known earlier, he would have made that call sooner and apologized for all this extra distress that it caused me.

I asked him what he thought of me going for another opinion, and he said that it's up to me and he'll be there no matter which doctor I would switch to. Because it's such a rare case and there's very minimal information about it, if it'll calm me down to hear another opinion I should go for it, but there's no medical reason to get a second opinion.

My parents were very concerned about me. They saw how scared I was, they knew I wasn't eating well, and they saw me in pain. They felt very strongly that I should go for another opinion. As much as I dreaded and disliked going to the MFM that I was seeing, I couldn't see myself having to be told all this negative information all over again. I thanked my parents for their advice and chose to decline it.

My husband started obsessing about the diagnosis, the size, and what it would be like. He was catastrophizing this situation, and it was really causing him a lot of emotional distress.

In the meantime, my hands and fingers were very tingly and numb, which was painful. I didn't know what it was. At first, I thought maybe it was the way I slept, but when it wasn't going away and only getting worse, I spoke to the Doctor about it. She said I have carpal tunnel.

I went to OT/PT once a week for the rest of the pregnancy, and it relieved the pain while I was there. However, when I got home, I didn't feel any progress. I would sleep in a hand brace, switch between ice packs and heating pads, and do some exercises to release some of the pain and tingles, which worked for the moment.

The results from the amniocentesis procedure came back. Everything was good, thank G-D! We were very grateful! I continued with this MFM until I was seven months pregnant, and at that point, she told me that I'd be transferred over to their team in Manhattan. The MFM told me that the team in Manhattan is more experienced and well equipped, and I'll no longer be seeing her. What a relief! I can breathe again!

Though nervous about meeting the new team of doctors, I spoke up for myself right away. They knew why I was there as they had gotten all my medical records, but I told them I wanted to know what was going on. The truth is, there was no need to hide any details, but I did need some sensitivity. Even though I knew it was a catastrophic situation, I tried to stay positive. I met the new team of doctors. They were a lot more understanding, sensitive, and informative than the previous MFM. They eagerly wanted our case as it was so rare. It was a great learning experience for the doctors. I asked them if my ob-gyn could be present at my birth, to which they said no. The policy in the hospital is that only the doctor from the team can be present and I can have one person with me, which would be my husband.

I asked them if I could have a natural birth, and they said so long as the baby was not breached, I could have a natural delivery. I davened (prayed) that this baby should not breach. By the appointments I was updated that the baby is not breached, it was in the perfect position for natural delivery. I felt very positive about that. I knew my life was about to change. We were expecting the worst, but at least I could have a natural birth.

They had us meet the surgeon who would be on the baby's case, and he told us the baby can survive though we don't know what the outcome would be. My husband very nervously asked him if we were going to have to have a handicapped accessible vehicle. He said I don't have answers to that right now, though we should mentally prepare ourselves that we may need to get a handicapped vehicle. We may also need to be on a level floor in the house as this child may not be mobile. Being that it was near the kidneys, it may affect the child's ability to use the bathroom and may affect breathing. The baby may need to be hooked onto machines, and the images were not clear, so they weren't sure if it would affect the spine. All this was speculation as there was no way to know until after birth.

He predicted that if the baby makes it, they'll keep the baby monitored in the hospital for the first three to six months and then possibly do some interventions.

The meeting was over, and we went back home. It was a lot to swallow. I called my ob-gyn and discussed this all with him. He reassured me that he was praying for us. We should continue to stand strong, and the doctors say the worst to cover themselves. We should listen to them, and also know it can be exaggerated.

In the meantime, my father was speaking to a close, well-respected family relative and told him the situation. He advised us to go for a second opinion. My father called me and tried convincing me to go for another opinion. I told him I understood why I should but I'm comfortable in my environment, and it's hard to change and start the whole process all over again.

My father persisted, he didn't give up and kept asking me to reconsider and just go for a second opinion. After a while, he told me to make an appointment.

He said he would take me so my husband wouldn't need to miss any more work. I didn't want to, though I agreed. I told my husband and said I'm not switching doctors; I'm just going for Kibud Av (honoring my father) and to make my father happy.

It was Friday, a month before my due date. My father drove and came along with me to the hospital for a second opinion. We waited a short while and were greeted very warmly by the nurses and doctors.

The doctor called me in and spoke with me. I told them everything from the beginning up until this point. They examined me and did imaging. When they were done, they told me what they saw, and they were a lot more optimistic about the situation. They said, it's up to me whether I wanted to switch over to them or not. Though it's very important that you know, you cannot have a natural delivery, it will have to be a caesarian section.

I was in shock, I told them the other doctor said I could have a natural delivery so long as the baby was not breached. They went on to explain that for my own safety if G-D forbid I were to start delivering naturally, it can put my life and the baby's life in danger. The baby can get stuck, tear me completely open, and have trouble getting out.

After this was all explained to me, I understood it was going to be a C- section. I'm not going to take any risks.

The doctors all sat around together with my father and I and explained everything with lots of hope for the baby. They then had me meet with their surgeon, who told me the plans based on the images, what he saw, and thought would be done. He said there are different types of surgeries the baby may need. After birth, they'll evaluate the baby to see when it had to be done and have more answers.

I thanked my father for taking me and convincing me to go for this second opinion. I spoke it over with my husband, and we decided to switch over to this team. If the other doctors were willing to let me give birth naturally and didn't see the dangers in that, it was a big red flag. It meant that they were really not knowledgeable, and I wasn't going to take a chance.

We made the switch. My husband was very impressed with the doctors, and we were happy and felt we had made the right decision. We were seen, and they had us come back the next Friday as well. They then said we should schedule to meet with the rest of the team. We had an appointment for Monday to meet with the MFM, ob-gyn, and some other doctors.

On Monday, they checked me, and I was dilated a little. They spoke with me and said Thursday, you'll be thirty-eight weeks. We don't want you to give birth before then. However, we have to plan a date for delivery. They said it can be anytime between Thursday to Tuesday.

Motzei Shabbos (Saturday night) was Shavous (Shavuot, a Jewish Holiday) until Monday night. Being a mother and thinking of my family, I said let's plan for Tuesday. This way I'll have the last Shabbos (Shabbat) and Yom Tov (holiday) with my children before our world turns chaotic.

The doctors checked the schedule and said they were fully booked on Tuesday, that won't work out. Being that it was planned I didn't want to schedule the birth on Shabbos or Yom Tov (holiday) and I wasn't even sure if I was allowed to. So, my next options were either Thursday or Friday. I said let's do it Thursday night after I get all my kids to sleep. They looked at me and said, being that it's a more complex situation, we prefer it first thing in the morning so the doctor is fully alert, has enough energy, and will be refreshed to deliver the baby. So, with that being said, we scheduled a C-section for Thursday.

The next day, we came back to meet with the plastic surgeon, and we told her what was going on. We informed her that we were scheduled for delivery on Thursday. She couldn't believe it, and said she was in shock. She had a planned vacation for ten days to another country, leaving on Friday. And she was so happy that she'd be there by the birth.

Hashem really orchestrates everything perfectly to the tee. I wanted the baby to be born Tuesday, though it didn't work out in our favor. Hashem knew best that this baby should be born on Thursday so all doctors and surgeons could be present! Thank you, Hashem (G-D)!

CHAPTER: 5

Diagnosis:

O ur child was diagnosed with an Abdominal Lymphatic Malformation. What is that? It's lymphatic vessels that are not properly formed. The malformations are lymphatic tissue filled with fluid (cysts). These lymphatic vessels are part of the lymphatic system, which is part of the immune system, which helps fight diseases and infections. It also maintains the balance of the fluid in the body. It does this by emptying extra fluid into blood vessels.

Our princess was born with an abundance of cysts, some very enlarged and others microscopic, which cannot be addressed at the moment. The microscopic cysts can grow and enlarge at any given moment, like a volcano that's about to erupt.

When the cysts inflame, they can grow enormous, and if it's not treated, they can cause cellulitis infection, which can become very life threatening. When the cyst gets angry and starts acting out and growing, it can get out of control and won't stop on its own. It needs intervention, and most importantly prayers.

How does it happen? We were told by the doctors it is unknown; the baby was conceived healthy, and somewhere along the way, there was a fluke, and the lymphatic system went out of whack. Nothing I did or didn't do caused it or could've prevented it from happening.

We know and believe there's no such thing as a fluke; everything that happens is the will of Hashem (G-D), and for whatever reason, this child has to go through it along with us. We have to be the parents of this child, and my other children have to be the siblings. There's no such thing as coincidence, and we all need this in order for us to fulfill our tikun (mission) in life.

How common is this? 5% of people worldwide have Lymphatic Malformation, and of that 5%, less than 1% have it in the abdomen.

Can I see a picture of what it will look like? I get very oozy when I see blood and different things. I've vomited and fainted in the past. They had no pictures to show me of an Abdominal lymphatic malformation, though they showed me a picture of lymphatic malformation in another area of the body. I googled it myself as well and found it only in other areas. I felt very lightheaded and nauseous from taking a small glance at it.

- Will this affect the child cognitively? Unknown
- How will it affect the child's day to day life? Unknown
- Will the child be able to walk and talk? Unknown
- Will the child look normal? Unknown
- Will the child be able to live a regular lifestyle? Unknown
- Will the child function like others around them? Unknown
- How long will the child be hospitalized for? Unknown

These were a handful of the many, many questions we've asked. The doctors didn't have answers. It was unknown! The fear of the unknown was very frightening and real! It played a major factor in that we didn't have the proper resources to mentally prepare ourselves. It gave us too much head space to imagine and expect the worst possible outcome. It put a massive strain on us both mentally and physically. The number of questions, thoughts, and worries that arose due to the unknown was piling up more and more as the days moved along.

We wanted to plan ahead of time to try to keep our family intact, healthy, stable, and functioning within the challenge we were about to be faced with.

The unknown was very complex. It's challenging to make arrangements and plan the future of our children without having answers! We wanted to keep the family together and strong! We were hoping to keep routines in our home environment together so my children's lives wouldn't turn into chaos. It was important that they can be healthy and normal within these circumstances! However, we couldn't plan ahead of time since there was no knowledge and no time frame given to us! The fear of the unknown was very alive!

We have a concept of Emunah and Bitachon (Belief/Faith and Trust) in Hashem (G-D). The more we believe and trust that everything that happens is for the best and Hashem has a plan, the less room we have to worry and be afraid. We know we don't understand G-D, and we don't have to. All we have to know is that God is perfect, and everything He does is perfect, even when it doesn't seem that way through the limited vision of the human eye. However, the more we hold on to this strong belief and trust in Hashem (G- D), the less room we have to worry.

We've always believed Hashem (G-D) only gives us what we can handle. I couldn't understand what was happening. How would I bear a baby that I wouldn't be able to look at? How would I be able to take care of such a baby? I didn't understand. Though I knew and believed Hashem would only give me what I could handle, I was still very scared to see the baby. This was very frightening. I knew that a baby like this would need lots of extra love and care, and I didn't know if I was capable or what it was going to be like.

The whole pregnancy, "Tatty My King" was my song. It gave me chizuk (strength), life, and hope. This is what kept me going, through all my fears and worries of the unknown, I knew Hashem (G-D) was with me at every moment. Not a second goes by that G-D is not holding onto me.

I kept encouraging myself saying Hashem put me through it. Hashem will guide me and hold me through it! Hashem will give me all the courage and strength I need to get through the whole situation! When I was six months pregnant, people started asking me if I was due any day, if I was overdue, and when I was due. I didn't want to tell people my due date, because I was told all the way in the beginning that they may put me in labor early depending on the status of the baby.

It was very hard for me to walk as I was carrying a lot of extra weight from the baby's condition, and I was retaining water in my legs. I walked around waddling. I would go to the bus stop with my children, which was less than a minute walk. By the time I got home, I was huffing and puffing, out of breath as if I had just run a marathon. I had a hard time getting up and down and switching from one position to another.

I bathed my children every night, and one night I was not feeling up to it. I told my kids that we would skip baths. They looked at me so surprised and said Mommy, you want us to be smelly kids? I felt terrible. I called my mother and Baruch Hashem (Blessed is G-D) she came to save the day!

When I was home, I tried to do everything I possibly could by myself. I felt so bad relying on favors, and with all my appointments I needed it, so I didn't want to take advantage.

As I entered my seventh month, people started asking me if I was expecting multiples. I was carrying really big, and I had very little energy. Emotionally and physically, I was drained! I knew how I looked, so I understood why people thought I was carrying multiples. Plus, I carried much smaller with my other four children.

I avoided going to outside gatherings and social events, as emotionally I was very vulnerable and didn't want to be seen, and I wasn't interested in having to deal with all these comments.

This gave me a greater sensitivity towards others. I won't ask or assume that someone is expecting. If they are, I'll wait until they are ready to tell me. You never know what's going on, and saying the most obvious thing can cause sharp pain when someone is going through hardships.

We all have difficulties in life in all different aspects and ways. No two people experience pain in the same way. I saw firsthand how my husband and I were going through the same challenge, yet we both handled it completely differently. Not only that, we also couldn't understand each other's way of dealing with the situation. During the pregnancy, instead of embracing the moments to bring us closer together, we put distance between us and drifted apart.

It came to the end of the pregnancy after we had already scheduled the birth, and we had a very intense talk. He was in fight or flight mode the whole pregnancy, so I told him if we didn't work things out and he couldn't get a handle on himself and be there for me, then I didn't want him to come to the birth with me.

He was not expecting that to come from me, though I explained I'm very emotional and vulnerable. I need support, and if you can't be supportive, I'll get support from my mother. He took it to heart and apologized. He really felt bad for the way he had been acting and started making a shift in his behaviors. He wanted to make up for all the extra stress and distress he caused.

We made plans for all the kids to stay from Thursday through Motzei Shavuos (After the end of Shavuot). We got home from a meeting with a plastic surgeon on Wednesday and headed out to a restaurant with the family as our last fun memory before the baby was born. We told the kids I was going to the hospital to have a baby, and we told them where they were going to be staying. After we settled back at home and put the kids to bed, we got a call that the plans fell through for two of my children.

Nervous as can be for tomorrow, I couldn't think straight. Now we need to make new arrangements for two of our children. I had a friend that I called and just burst into tears, telling her the situation I was in. She was so understanding and offered to come early in the morning before I left so my toddler could warm up to her. She came with her toddler and stayed the entire day watching my kids. She was there as they came home from school. She fed them dinner, and stayed until they were picked up to go to where they were staying.

At the moment, I felt hopeless and stuck, but in the end, as always, everything fell into place! The key is to stay strong until you get to that point.

Reflecting back on the pregnancy:

What gave us the courage to stand strong and not terminate the pregnancy when the MFM was persuasively trying to convince us to terminate? We stood strong to our gut feelings, beliefs, values, and morals. The thought that popped into my head as soon as the doctor brought it up was, I'm not a murderer, and what if the doctors are wrong? What if there's a turning point in the pregnancy, and the baby becomes healthy? How can I take a life away that G-D is granting to live? And I'd never be able to live within myself knowing I took life away from another soul.

When you set a strong foundation of values and beliefs nothing and no one can convince you to say or do anything that doesn't fit into your value and belief system! If you don't have a strong foundation of values and beliefs, it's never too late. You can start now. Think of values you appreciate, study them, research them, understand them and then gradually incorporate them into your life. As you start learning to appreciate your values and beliefs, you'll become more passionate about them, and that will help you stand up for what you truly believe in.

Doctors are more knowledgeable than you. Why didn't you go along with how they were guiding you? Yes, doctors are more educated, and they spend a lot more time in school learning, researching, and practicing. G-D granted us with an intuition and a gut feeling, which should not be the decision alone, but it has to be taken into full consideration. A mother knows their child best. Even if I don't know the protocol, treatments, etc. I know when something doesn't seem right.

It's very important to always ask doctors questions, make sure you understand the diagnosis, the treatment and everything they are going to be doing. Make sure you understand the way they speak. If they use too much medical language that you don't understand, don't be shy. Ask them to explain it in a way that you can understand. Don't be scared to ask or disagree, as you are your child's best advocate.

At the end of the day, doctors are human beings. No matter how good they are or what their reputation is, they can make mistakes. G-D is the ultimate Doctor/Healer. Doctors are the messengers of G-D to take care of your medical needs. I always pray that whichever doctor, resident, surgeon, or nurse is taking care of my daughter, they should be the perfect messenger and it should be without any complications.

How did we cope and function with the constant negativity? Emotionally, it was painful and draining. Lots of tears were shed and lots of prayers were cried and spoken. I connected with a song that gave me hope and strength.

Did we actually want the baby? Yes, we knew this child would be a special, unique and holy soul. We feel privileged and gifted to be the parents chosen for this baby.

Without such a strong support system, how were you able to function? I was thinking of the baby. I took myself out of the picture. If it was about me, it would have been an impossible situation. I gave it all I got for our baby.

When you were told about the diagnosis, how did you feel? We were scared, nervous, and worried, but at the same time felt extremely grateful and praiseful to G-D that it was nothing worse.

CHAPTER: 6

June 6, 2019

After a restless night's sleep, I packed everyone for the next couple of days. I got up bright and early, dressed and fed the children, and gave them big hugs and kisses as I was going to miss them. The three bigger kids went to school, my friend came to take care of my toddler, and shortly after we headed out.

On the way, we had a lot of time to talk and reflect back on this journey that we each did solely. We heard each other out, and my husband promised to be there for me all the way.

I shared my worries, concerns, and fears, and he shared his. He was being very supportive and gave me lots of reassurance. He was excited to take part in the next chapter of life together with me. We finally connected on an emotional level for the first time since the news was broken to us the day of the twenty-week anomaly scan.

I remember leaving the car and walking into the hospital, knowing I was going to be giving birth but not in labor. I've never experienced that before, and it felt very strange. We signed in and waited in the waiting area for a couple of minutes until they called me into the triage.

My mother came and met us at the perfect time. Moments after she arrived, a resident came in to introduce herself and told me she would be delivering my baby. I said it's nice to meet you, thank you! Though I'm going to have an actual doctor deliver me. I know my baby's situation is unknown, and I'm not having any mess ups with the delivery. She said the doctor would be in the room overlooking the site, but she would do the C-section. I told her I'm sorry, I'm not signing the papers, I want the doctor.

We had a connection to get into the hospital with a close family relative/friend. Right away, my mother called him up and spoke with him. Within ten minutes, he called her back up to let us know not to worry. The doctor would do the delivery, not a resident. A few minutes later, a doctor came, gave me a hug, and asked how I was doing. Right away I said I really hope you're delivering my baby. She looked at me and said you don't want me to deliver the baby, I'm the plastic surgeon. Being that I had only met these doctors once before, I recognized them, but I didn't remember who was who. We all had a nice, good laugh. A few minutes after that, the doctor came with the consent forms and informed us that she got the message and reassured us that she'd be delivering the baby. At that point, I signed the consent form and thanked her very much!

The nurse came and did my vitals, and I asked if I could have both my mother and husband in the operating room. They said only one person can come with me, so my mother was told to wait in the triage. I went to the OR and my husband joined me shortly after.

I got in my hospital gown and hat, and they walked me to the OR, though they didn't let my husband come in at the time. I was very scared as I peeked into the OR. I stopped before I entered the room and said this is really scary. They asked what was scary. I looked around and pointed to all the machinery, doctors, and nurses in the room. I said all of this is very scary and I didn't know what I'm getting myself in to.

They said they were going to give me a spinal, and after they're done, they'll allow my husband in the room. They also said if I was in too much pain with the spinal, they would have to put me under anesthesia, and I told them no way!

She was about to give me the spinal, and I looked at her and said, you're so young. I asked her for her age, and I was relieved to know she was a bit older than me. Then I gave the go ahead, and I said some Tehillim (Psalms) that I knew by heart as she gave me a spinal.

The spinal was done, and my husband came into the room. With his presence, I felt a lot safer. He sat by my side, holding my hand tight. They put a big curtain over me, so we couldn't see what was going on.

As they began, I gave a big shout, "oww, ouch, that hurts". They asked what it felt like, and I said I felt like I got poked with a knife. They said the spinal didn't work. They did it in the wrong spot and had to redo it. She redid the spinal as I said some more Tehillim (Psalms), this time with my husband at my side.

When the spinal was in correctly, I looked around the room with my husband. There were nineteen doctors and nurses in the room, eighteen females and one male. I asked why there's so many people they explained who each person was. We had the ob-gyn team, plastic surgery team, anesthesiologists team, NICU team, and some nurses in the room.

They began the C-section, and I was squeezing my husband's hand so tight. I was filled with so many mixed emotions. My carpel tunnel acted up, and my hands swelled so badly that they literally doubled in size. I was uncomfortable from the C-section, my hands were numb and tingling uncontrollably, and I was in pain. It took them forty-five minutes, and they said congratulations, you had a baby! I was so weak, and the first thing I asked was if the baby was okay. Is the baby breathing? Is it a boy or a girl? The nurse standing to the side of me said she'd go find out.

Moments later, she came back and said congratulations, you had a baby girl. The baby is breathing on her own, though they took her straight to the NICU to monitor and check her. I asked the ob-gyn how much longer and when I would be done, and she said she needed a few more minutes to put my organs back into place and close me back up.

I was so weak, I was emotionally and physically worn, torn and drained. The placenta was out, and I was closed up. I asked if I could go straight to the NICU to meet my baby. They said my blood pressure dropped really low, and they put me on medicine to help my blood pressure get back to normal. In the meantime, I have to go straight to the high-risk room to continue with my IV fluids and to be monitored.

I asked if my baby could be brought to me so I could see and meet her. They said the baby is going to have an MRI done, and we'll have a race. If I'm discharged from the high-risk room first, I'll go straight to the NICU, and if the baby goes for an MRI first, she'll come to me on the way.

In the meantime, my husband went to the NICU to meet our precious gem for the very first time. He took some pictures to show me. When he saw our daughter's abdominal lymphatic malformation, his reaction was how can G-D give me such a hideous looking creature. A NICU doctor looked at my husband and said, "You're going to walk this princess down the aisle, I promise." My husband thought something was up with that doctor. How would it be possible to walk such a hideous looking body down the aisle? He continued to look at her, thinking the face was beautiful and perfect, but the body just didn't match up. It caused my husband to feel very sad, and he had a lot of questions.

He just couldn't understand what G-D was thinking when he created our child. He asked Hashem (G-D) to please give him a sign that we are in His hands, and He has a master plan.

My husband came to show me the pictures, and I saw the most beautiful princess. I couldn't stop crying as I was looking at the picture and thinking what a miracle she was. This was the most beautiful princess that they were trying to convince me to abort.

Hodu LaHashem Ki Tov Ki Lolom Chasdo (Thank G-D for His goodness because His grace is forever). I was so emotional and thankful to Hashem for giving me the most precious gift. And I was anxiously waiting to meet her.

The plastic surgeon came in to check on how I was doing, and I couldn't utter a word out of my mouth. I just poured out in tears, crying like a baby. She told me that the baby is beautiful and is being very well monitored by a great team of doctors and nurses.

A little while later, some residents came to us explaining that until the baby goes for an MRI, they will not be feeding her, and they wanted to insert a pic line for them to feed her through. At the time, I didn't understand the difference between a pic line and a regular IV line. They explained it to us and said to think about it and someone would be back shortly with consent forms to fill out.

We discussed it and agreed to it. They came back, I signed the consent forms, and told them to send lots of hugs to my princess, who I was eagerly awaiting to meet. I asked if there was any update on what time the baby was going in for an MRI, and they informed me that they were waiting for a time slot to open up.

My father came to pick up my mother, so he waited with us as everyone was eager to meet her. They only let my husband in the NICU. We all waited and waited impatiently. I kept asking the nurse who was taking care of me when I'd be out since all I wanted was to meet my baby, they said it's up to when my numbers are okay, so we just have to continue waiting patiently.

It was getting later on in the day and there were still no updates with the timing for the MRI. In the meantime, I requested my own room for when I get admitted. We had to wait for a room to be available. We asked if we could get our own room without a roommate, and they said it's possible, though the chances of it becoming available are slim as there are lots more rooms with roommates.

I wanted my own room so my husband could stay and be together with me for Shabbos (Shabbat) through Shavuos (Shavuot Holiday). If not, he promised to sleep on the benches of the west side highway to be with me. As it was a three-day holiday, we Orthodox Jews refrain from laboring and using any sort of electricity, so commuting from Brooklyn was not an option.

It was already 11:15 p.m. with no updates. It was getting late, and my parents were still there. They wanted to stay to see the baby, but they were getting tired, and their commute home was over an hour. We all knew how badly they wanted to meet my princess, though they were exhausted. My mother had been there since around 12:00 noon. It was a long, overwhelming, exhausting, and emotional day. They decided to wait a few more minutes. By 11:45 p.m. they said their good nights, wished us the best, gave us some Brachos (Blessings), and they left. At about 12:20 a.m., the NICU team came into my room with the most precious, beautiful, miraculous princess. I was still numb from the spinal, I couldn't move, and my legs felt paralyzed. I asked if they could put the baby on my lap. I wanted to hold her, hug, and kiss her. They said they didn't want anyone lifting her because her body was very weak and fragile, and they were scared she could get hurt. So, they put the basin next to me and I stretched out my arms and rubbed her arms and spoke to her and told her how much I love her. They let me be with her for about two minutes, and they had to go to the MRI. As soon as she left, I broke down. I was so happy that I got to meet my princess, though it was an empty feeling when they walked out of the room with her. I was so sad and emotional. I wanted to be there for my baby and couldn't. It was emotionally a very painful experience.

Around 12:45 a.m., they came in with great news. A single room had just become available, meaning I could have that room for just me and my husband with a couch that opens into a bed. This felt like such a big hug from Hashem. My husband gathered up all our belongings, and they took me out in a wheelchair. We couldn't believe our eyes when we got to our room, a single room, and it was room number 613! Why was 613 so special to us at this very moment? It was because we were about to approach the holiday of Shavuos (Shavuot), which is a celebration of receiving the Torah (Bible) at Har Sinai (Mount Sinai). The Torah has 613 Mitzvos (commandments). So, the number 613 represents the commandments. It's a unique and special number.

At this moment, my husband felt very relieved. He got the sign and understood that Hashem was completely by our side and was guiding us through this. This was no coincidence, and we understood the baby was perfect. We had to be patient and daven (pray) a lot for the health and cure of our princess. We felt the light shining on us and knew Hashem was on our team! This was a great kiss from Hashem (G-D)! Wow! What a day! What a long eighteen weeks, where every day something cropped up. It was eighteen weeks filled with mystery, fears, emotions, pain, strength, and reliance on Hashem (G-D). We couldn't believe we made it to this very point. We still felt nervous and scared, though we were excited and relieved that Chasdei Hashem (With the kindness of G-D), we had made it to this point, and we were looking forward to starting the next chapter in our lives and conquering the unknown!

CHAPTER: 7

After a restless night's sleep and feeling incomplete from missing my precious princess, I just wanted to be by her side, we were woken up with some updated news that the MRI results came in. Baruch Hashem (Blessed is G-D) the spine and heart were fine, though the lymphatic was touching the outskirts of the kidneys, which was very concerning to the doctors. Her digestive system was working Baruch Hashem (Blessed is G-D), so she could start with bottle feedings. We felt so blessed and had an enormous amount of gratitude towards Hashem (G-D). Yet we were all davening (praying) for her and felt nervous about the kidneys.

After this news, I was more anxiously waiting to go visit our princess in the NICU.

All I saw was her beautiful face, as her body was covered in a blanket. I was scared to see her body and was not ready to look. We informed all the doctors and nurses that I was not ready to see the baby's body, so when I was around, her body should be fully covered. They were very understanding and supportive. They told me I should take my time, and as soon as I feel ready, I should be exposed to it very gradually and slowly.

As I was in a lot of pain, very weak, and I still couldn't walk, the nurse wheeled me to the NICU, and we were there for a few minutes. I was kissing her, rubbing her arms and face, talking, and saying Tehillim (Psalms). I spoke to her and apologized that she was going through so much pain, and that I couldn't be there with her. I told her I was always going to be there for her as much as I possibly could. She is my world! I kissed her and got ready to head back to my room.

My husband lifted the blanket and couldn't stop staring at her mass, he was studying the size, shape and coloring. He couldn't stop staring and obsessing about the abdominal lymphatic malformation (LM). It looked like a mass. The surface of the skin was red, purple and blue. It was very swollen and fragile.

Her birth weight was 11lbs. 14oz. That was due to her lymphatic malformation. It was on the right side of her body. It looked like the size of a big, huge watermelon. She couldn't fit into the baby's hospital gown, so they'd just cover her with the hospital's receiving blankets, and they'd take two size five diapers and put one on in the front and one in the back and connect the two as one big diaper.

Being that it was so big, she was only able to lie on her back. They didn't allow anyone to hold her. They gave her a special foam mattress so that she wouldn't get back sores.

We headed back to our room, and as I was in a lot of pain from birth, they gave me some Motrin and Percocet. This was the first time in my life I've ever taken Percocet. It made me feel very spacey and out of it.

There was a knock on our door, and this woman introduced herself saying that she was from the genetic team, and they were doing research. She started reading to me from some of the papers that she was holding and was talking nonstop. I was so out of it. Everything she was saying went right over my head. At one point, I burst into laughter. I had such a laughing attack that was very contagious that my husband started laughing, and so did she. This went on for a few minutes. I finally got a hold of myself and stopped laughing. At that point my husband asked me what was so funny. I apologized for laughing as she was speaking, and I told her the Percocet kicked in. I didn't know what was flying. I told her it would be best for her to come back later when I don't have any Percocet in my system. She caught me at the wrong time and place.

A few hours later we got the birth certificate though we couldn't fill it out without a name. We began discussing names for our precious princess. We were not sure if we needed to add a name with the meaning of life, or healing, or if we can choose any name. My husband got in touch with our Rabbi. Being that she was able to breathe on her own, her life is not considered endangered, and we can choose any name we'd like.

The entire pregnancy we didn't find out the gender, and we didn't discuss names as we weren't sure what the situation would be. Now that it was Friday, we wanted to name our baby on Shabbos (Shabbat).

I don't know why, but the name Shalva kept popping up in my head throughout the pregnancy. It's a beautiful name that I really love, and it means tranquility. I told my husband, and he said it sounds beautiful, but he's never heard of that name. He called his Rabbi to confirm that it was a name, and it was, in fact, a real name. I told him he could choose a second name. He started coming up with so many names, and either I didn't like it, or it didn't flow nicely together with Shalva. He then said what about Nechama, which means comfort. I loved the meaning and agreed to the name.

Now we weren't sure which name should be first. I suggested we both imagine that she's here with us and we're calling her name. Back and forth we were both saying, Shalva Nechama, Nechama Shalva, Nechama Shalva, Shalva Nechama. We both liked how Shalva Nechama sounded better.

We spoke to our children and told them, "Mazel Tov! (Congratulations!) we had a baby girl!" We didn't tell the kids anything that was going on with our baby, because we weren't going to be with them and didn't want them to be scared. They were excited with the news that they had a new baby sister!

There was a knock on the door, and a woman introduced herself as a Chai Lifeline social worker volunteer. She handed over a really refreshing smoothie and danish pastry. She then spoke with me for a little while and told me that she'd be there for me every step of the way.

There are amazing Jewish organizations that provide food to those in the hospital. Being that we only eat strictly Kosher food, this was a big help during our stay. Otherwise, we would have had very minimal options for kosher hospital food.

We were fully stocked for Shabbos (Shabbat) and Shavuos (Shavuot). Between Chai Lifeline, Satmar, Bikur Cholim, and Chesed 24 (names of some of the amazing organizations) we were covered regarding food, drinks, pastries, snacks, cutlery, tablecloths, magazines, newspapers, and flowers. They went above and beyond to think of everything that might be needed so that we would not go hungry and feel as much at home as possible in the hospital room. They wanted to make sure we had a nice Shabbos (Shabbat) and Yom Tov (holiday) experience!

We felt so proud to be a part of the Jewish nation. These are strangers we've never met, didn't know, and they went way above anything anyone can think of to provide us with everything we would need. From emotional support, to lodging near the hospital to meals, rides, etc. They're incredible! We have such Hakaros Hatov (Gratitude) towards these organizations.

With all the hospitality that we were given during the stay in the hospital, and with the baby in the NICU, there were many mixed emotions. Our hospital stay was during the measles outbreak. Therefore, the hospital had a rule that there could only be the same three visitors for the patient during the entire hospital stay. And everyone had to show proof that they had the measles vaccine.

The three that we chose were me, my husband, and my mother. My mother and husband took the vaccine as they didn't have their old records. Since I was admitted, they gave me a choice. They can check my blood to see if I'm immune to the measles, or they can give me a vaccine. I knew I was up to date with all my vaccines, so I opted for them to check my blood.

On Shabbos morning, my husband went to daven (pray). They had a minyan (The quorum of 10 men gathered together to pray) in the family room of the hospital. It was very generous for the hospital to allow us to use the family room for prayers during the holidays.

It was a very warm and emotional experience for my husband. It was the first time in his life to come and pray together with all different types of Jewish men from all different backgrounds, unified as one. With each and every individual having their own story to share, we were all here praying in the hospital family room. It brought me to tears. I felt such a connection with all my fellow brethren.

In our Jewish tradition, we announce the baby's name by prayers when we are called up to read from the Torah. At this point, our baby was officially named Shalva Nechama in the hospital family room. It was a very emotional experience for all that were present. And they all wished her a blessing of Refuah Shelaima (Healing and speedy recovery).

When the men were done with the prayers, my husband and I went straight to the NICU to visit our daughter Shalva Nechama. We then told the nurses and doctors the name as well, and everyone loved it. We told them we would be calling her Shalva. Child Life made a nice name sign and hung it on top of her basin. We stayed in the NICU for a few minutes and then headed up to our room to have the Shabbos seudah (meal).

As we were eating the meal together, we were reflecting back on the past twenty-four hours and really appreciated that we had the full Shabbos experience with everything you can think of. At the same time there was a big emptiness inside of me from missing my baby Shalva. I just wanted Shalva in my arms, and I wanted to be in her presence. My husband sang Shabbos zemiros (Shabbat songs), and then we bentched (blessings said at the conclusion of a meal).

We headed straight back to the NICU to Shalva. I just thanked Hashem for her gorgeous face, the most beautiful big blue eyes, and long eyelashes. I sang to her, talked to her, and prayed for her. Every doctor, resident, nurse, and passerby who saw Shalva couldn't stop talking about how beautiful she was, and her eyes stood out to everyone!

When my husband wanted to look at her Mass (that's what we called the lymphatic malformation), I would walk away. He would stare and literally tried analyzing if the mass grew, stayed the same or shrunk, if the coloring was better or worse and how it felt. He tried discussing it with me and I would start feeling oozy.

When we were in my room, I was saying Tehillim (psalms), and I just broke into tears. I felt so helpless for Shalva. I wanted to be there for her, and there was nothing I could do. I shared my feelings with my husband, and he reassured me that praying for her was the best thing I could possibly do to help her, and G-D is in control! G-D can cure her! I felt good hearing that, and I believed that, but that empty feeling was still eating me up.

We went back to visit Shalva and being that the blood work didn't come back regarding my immunity towards measles, they handed me over a mask. I felt very claustrophobic, so I stayed with Shalva for a few minutes and then headed back to our room.

In the meantime, a resident updated us that over the weekend, they are just going to be monitoring her and doing some blood work and continue bottle feeding her. At this time, they gave me great news. I couldn't nurse as no one could hold her, but I could pump bottles for her. I was very excited about that. Pumping around the clock is not an easy task, though I cherished every moment of it. I felt so blessed to be able to nurture my baby. Besides singing, talking, massaging her, and praying for her, there was not much more that I was able to do.

As the holiday was nearing an end, I started feeling very sad. I knew that I was being discharged that night. I couldn't see myself leaving Shalva behind. I broke down in uncontrollable tears and cried out to Hashem. I tried to self-talk and to accept the situation. I tried reassuring myself that Shalva was in good hands and that I'd be back the very next morning. In the meantime, I'd get to see and be with the rest of my children.

Over Shavous, my husband spent hours walking on the George Washington Bridge. He had lots of time to think and reflect on everything that's been going on. It created lots of insecurity, fear, and anxiety.

By the time the holiday was over, he was walking back from the NICU with his shoulders down, dragging his feet. As he was heading back towards the room in the unit where we were staying, he bumped into another gentleman who was there. He just had a baby over the holiday. At that moment, he introduced himself as Rabbi Yudi Shmotkin. He said a warm hi and asked my husband his name and what brought him here. To which he responded that we had a baby. At that moment, my husband noticed he was a man who was all ears and ready to listen. He opened up, poured out his heart, and told him everything we'd been through.

CHAPTER: 8

As my husband finished telling Rabbi Shmotkin our story, the Rabbi gave him a big, warm hug. That was just the injection of love and faith he needed. He was the right man for my husband to see at the right time and place! It turns out that he is the Chabad Rabbi of Columbia University. The hug was the start of a relationship that will last forever.

The night was coming to an end, and we were discharged. We went to the NICU to spend more time with Shalva. We spoke to the resident doctors, and they promised to call us with all updates and won't proceed with doing anything without speaking to us first. They saw that we were sad, emotional, and devastated having to leave without Shalva. They reassured us that she was in great hands, and they gave us the nurse's station number so we could call to check in at any given time.

It was about 1:00 a.m. sad and heartbroken, I said some Tehillim (psalms), and Shema (a prayer said before going to sleep at night) with Shalva. I took some pictures and gave her a big hug and kiss. I promised I'd be back the next day. With that, we headed out.

We went straight to pick up one of our children that night. He was so excited to see us and to meet his new baby sister. He came into the car feeling very confused, asking where's Shalva? We told him she was not feeling so well and was going to stay in the hospital for a little bit. I showed him pictures of her face.

The next morning, the other three kids came home, and they ran into the house asking where the baby was. I then told them all that the baby was born with a booboo, so we kept her in the hospital. They had lots of questions. If she has booboo, how come we don't just put a band aid on it and let her come home? I explained it's a little bigger than that, and because she's so small and a newborn baby, it's safest that she stays in the hospital. They felt so bad for her and said they'd daven for her. I told them that children have such holy souls and Hashem loves the prayers of little children.

The new routine in the house was everyone woke up and got ready for school. While the kids were eating, I'd call the nurse's station to see how Shalva's night was and how she was doing. I asked if there were any changes or updates.

After the phone call, my kids asked me what the nurse said. I would just say, the baby is doing well and slept well overnight. They were not satisfied, they liked to know every single detail. So, I'd share more details with them.

After the kids would go to school, my husband would drop me off at the hospital and head back to work. I'd stay with Shalva all day in the NICU and leave every night. I tried to be home before my kid's bedtime so I could spend some time with them. I really wanted their lives to stay as normal and routinely healthy as possible. We'd talk about their day, and then we spent some time talking about Shalva. I had them all express their feelings and thoughts, and we all listened and tried to inspire each other. My children are my life, and I want them to all be happy and healthy.

Every few days, my children would ask if there were any updates about Shalva coming home. As they asked, I took those moments as opportunities to open up a little more about Shalva.

We are very into being open, straight up, and honest. We told our children nothing but the truth. We told them little by little, so they had time to digest it in a healthy manner. I didn't want to cause them any fear or anxiety, so I always spoke to them in a positive way.

When they asked to see pictures of the booboo, I told them I still hadn't seen it. I wanted to see it before we showed the kids pictures to make sure it was something they could handle.

Every Shabbos that she was in the hospital, I stayed with her from beginning to end. Sometimes my husband would stay with me, and we'd find places for my other children to go. Other times, he'd stay home with them, and my mother would accompany me.

The second Shabbos of Shalva's life my mother and I spent together with Shalva in the hospital. When it was over, my husband was on the way to pick me up. I decided to close the curtains and try leaning over the crib to nurse. Shalva had a great latch and nursed beautifully. I nursed her for the first time. I felt such a bond and connection with her. I was literally in tears when I had to go home.

Being that I didn't tell the nurses or doctors that I nursed Shalva Saturday night, when I came back Sunday, I asked them if I could nurse her. They got me a rocking chair and let me hold her with her mattress on my lap for the very first time when she was ten days old. I felt so emotionally overjoyed and happy. The emptiness was leaving, and I started feeling complete. There was nothing in the world like holding my princess for the very first time and being able to nurse and nurture her.

Up until this point, despite never having held her, I still loved her deeply. Yet, I felt a lingering sense of detachment, even though I spent every day by her bedside from morning until night. Getting to nurse her filled my heart with lots of happiness and joy. I cherished each moment. For the very first time, I felt I was her Mommy.

The NICU had some rules. One of them was not using your phone. As hard as it was sometimes, it was so beautiful that I really got to take in and spend every minute of quality time with Shalva. I would talk, sing, look, nurse, and massage her. When she was sleeping, I had lots of time to reflect, think, and appreciate my precious princess. I also had time to daven for her.

I'd be there every day when they came to do their rounds. I listened to everything they said, and I asked lots of questions. When they spoke amongst each other, they used lots of medical terms that I didn't understand. I'd ask them to explain it to me using regular simplified English so I can understand and be involved every step of the way. Before signing any consent forms or giving permission, I'd make sure I knew and understood everything. The first ten days in the hospital after birth, they were doing lots of monitoring, testing, blood work, imaging, and research until they finally came up with a plan. The teams of the plastic surgeon, pediatric surgeon, and radiologist, along with the residents and doctors, were all on board.

The plastic surgeon and attending doctor met with us in the NICU to discuss Shalva's situation and the plans for moving forward. After a little into the conversation, she told us that they were excited for Shalva to be their teacher. As soon as those words left her mouth, I burst into tears. On one hand, I respected and appreciated their honesty and humbleness. On the other hand, I was so scared and worried. I didn't want my princess to be the guinea pig.

That night, I was so emotional. We spoke a lot and discussed the situation with my parents, and they sent us the phone number of an organization that gives you resources and guides you to the best doctors for the diagnosis that you're dealing with.

I called and started speaking. After a minute of the phone call, I just burst out crying. I was so emotional I couldn't get a word out of my mouth. At that point, my husband took over the phone call, filled him in, and asked him to advise us what to do.

He strongly recommended we switch hospitals, and he said he'd help us with the transfer. My husband called the numbers he gave us, but they didn't accept our insurance. My husband updated him, and he gave us the number of an organization to help figure out insurance. My husband spoke to them, and it was very complex. They had lots of patience and tried to guide my husband through it. He tried but it wasn't working out in our favor.

In the meantime, as we were on the way to the hospital the next morning, we got a call from the well respectable Rabbi from the organization who was trying to help us switch hospitals. He said we should get a copy of the MRI and send the imaging to him right away so that he can send it to the doctors in the other hospital. As soon as we got to the hospital, we asked them for a CD of all the MRI and imaging they had. We waited a couple of minutes, and they handed it over to us. Being that we were nowhere near home and had to get the imaging over ASAP, my husband called Rabbi Yudi Shmotkin. He asked Rabbi Shmotkin if he was around and if he had a computer that we would be able to use to scan the CD and email it over. He immediately said sure and to go meet him at his office. We quickly hurried over. He stopped what he was doing and gave us all the time we needed to help us send these images over.

We then headed back to the hospital and told the surgeons and doctors how we felt and that we were looking into another hospital. They were very understanding. They offered to speak with the other teams of doctors before we made any decision.

We liked that idea, and the doctors all spoke. The plans they all had were the same for now.

My husband spoke to his Rabbi, updated him, and asked for advice. He also mentioned a concern that the hospital we are in is less than a one-and-a- half-hour ride from our house. Where the next hospital is, would not be commutable. This was a big concern we had as we didn't want to break up or split up the family. With all that information, the Rabbi said since both hospitals have the same plans, as of now stay where you are. So that's what we did.

The hospital was very happy to keep our case. They loved Shalva and were very warm and became like family. They always greeted me with hugs and nice smiles. They were very sensitive and understanding of all our worries and concerns.

They planned a meeting with all surgeons present for my husband, me, and our Rabbi. They spent a nice amount of time explaining everything all over again and took all our questions. We had lots of questions, but there were no answers. The humbler and more honest they were, the more comfortable we felt. That really reassured us that Hashem is the ultimate Doctor and the doctors and surgeons are just the messengers of G-D.

They discussed the plans of action, which they would start with a sclerotherapy treatment. Depending on how successful it would be, they'd either do another round of it or proceed with a debulking surgery (which we will elaborate on shortly). Being that the mass was the size of a big watermelon, they knew the game plan would be a lot more than Sclerotherapy.

They planned to do some intervention and start a round of Sclerotherapy treatment procedures. What is Sclerotherapy? Sclerotherapy is a procedure done in the Operating Room under anesthesia. The Interventional Radiologist injects a medication using needles into the lymph vessels and cysts. They have to target each individual cyst separately. What it's supposed to do is shrink the mass and destroy the walls of the cell so that it doesn't grow back. After the procedure was done, she would have drains connected to the pouch with shut off valves that they would drain and fill with medication for the next two days following the procedure.

Shalva was twelve days old, and I still hadn't looked at her Mass. I kept trying to talk myself into looking at it, and I knew I wanted to see it before any procedure was done. I decided to be brave and told the nurses I was not ready, but I would still like to see the mass before any intervention takes place. They advised that I wait until the surgeons, doctors, and the hospital social worker were present. We scheduled a time for everyone to be there including my husband.

The social worker came prepared with water, and she was talking very soothingly to me. Before they had me look at it, they told me to feel her mass over the blanket. Then, they slowly told me to touch her skin softly. I was focusing on my breathing and talking to Hashem to help me be able to see it without fainting or getting nauseous. While my husband was cheerleading me on, saying, you're so strong, you got until this point, you can do it, and the doctors and surgeons gave me lots of words of encouragement. They then showed me some pictures of it from different angles and slowly lifted up the entire blanket, and I saw her mass for the very first time.

Everyone clapped for me and was so proud that I handled it well. That's when I had a shiver down my spine. I realized that no matter how oozy I got about blood and all sorts of things, Hashem made sure to only give me what I could handle. That was such a good and relieving feeling.

After I saw it, I took some time to myself and really thanked Hashem for Shalva. I was so grateful and praiseful to Hashem that it was by her abdomen. Being that it was in that area of her body, Baruch Hashem, it didn't affect her heart, lungs, and other organs that would be critical to her health. I was also very grateful that it's a part of her body that is covered so that she would not have to walk around with any shame, embarrassment, judgment, and insecurity. I wanted her to be and feel like a regular, normal, healthy child without any labels or stigmas attached to her.

It was a long day, so my husband and I decided to go outside for some fresh air. We took a walk, and I shared all my thoughts with him. He appreciated it as well and we both felt the same. We were filled with lots of gratitude to Hashem! We continued to share all the blessings that we've been seeing and experiencing with each other.

I was privileged to have an amazing next-door neighbor who happens to be my sister-in-law. She stepped up to the plate and arranged with some family, neighbors, and friends that as long as Shalva was in the hospital my family would get gourmet dinners. Unless we were covered by Chai Lifeline.

When I gave birth to Shalva, I decided I wanted her diagnosis to be kept confidential. We only told our Rabbis and very close family. I didn't want any Ayin Hara (evil eye) or for Shalva to be the talk of the town. I also knew that nobody's ever heard of this diagnosis, and I wasn't up to being bombarded with tons of questions. We just told everyone that Shalva is in the hospital and needs lots of Tefillos. It was incredible to see that people really respected our privacy. They were very concerned and offered to help out in many different ways. It was an incredible feeling of achdus (unity).

We have not forgotten about how in the hospital Chai Lifeline would send us food every day. As well as come to visit and speak with me once a week. It was incredible to see how so many people care and will go out of their way to help.

CHAPTER: 9

My mother arrived at my house at 4:30 a.m. to babysit. We were headed off to the hospital for Shalva's Sclerotherapy procedure. I was full of nerves and scared for my little baby of fourteen days old to be put under anesthesia. I spread her name out for everyone to daven for her.

I walked beside her until we got to the OR room where I burst into tears. My precious baby was having a procedure. The doctor reassured me, and we waited by her bedside in the NICU, saying Tehillim the entire time.

An hour and a half later, the doctors brought Shalva back to me and told me everything went smoothly, and we will know if the procedure was successful after a couple of days. When we saw her after the procedure was over, we were already able to see that the mass had shrunk in size.

That day and the two following days, the Interventional Radiologist would insert medication into the valve, which is painful, irritating, and burning. To keep her out of pain, they gave her morphine. I was not comfortable with her constantly getting morphine, and I shared my concerns with the medical team, who heard and understood me. They discussed why they felt it was necessary, though they let me decide. We agreed that during the injections, she would get some morphine, as well as when she was in pain. After that, we would give her Motrin or Tylenol. I'd comfort her by holding her and nursing her.

After the third day, they came to take out the draining valve. They showed us that there was one liter (the size of a seltzer bottle) of fluid that came out.

We did this procedure for two weeks in a row, with three days of draining. Then they took a little break and kept her monitored. They did more blood work and imaging. We met with all the teams of doctors, and decided the next step would be to do the debulking surgery. We scheduled that for July 1st.

In the meantime, at home, the kids continued asking questions. They wanted to meet Shalva. Not a day went by without them asking when is Shalva coming home? When will we be able to meet our newborn baby sister? When I didn't have answers, they asked if they could come to the hospital to visit her.

We tried getting permission for them to visit, though because of the measles outbreak, they were super strict with visitors. Being that my kids were under eighteen, there was no chance. They told us they have a life center that's a fun, safe place for siblings to play with toys, arts and crafts. It also gave them time to snack and chat.

We made this into a routine of having the kids come to the hospital once a week. They really looked forward to it. During the snack and chat, they'd all have a chance to share their feelings and be heard. It was a safe place for them to ask questions. With their creativity, they made a manikin hooked onto an IV line with a booboo on the stomach to give the kids a little idea of what was going on. This made the kids feel included. They got a prize to take home, and they were told it was from Shalva.

After the first visit to the hospital was over, we packed into the minivan. We were listening to the Jewish radio station, and the most perfect song started playing at the perfect moment. It was a song by Yaakov Shwekey, "A Mother's Promise." We all listened quietly and let the words penetrate our hearts. It brought us all to tears. As we all understand, it was our journey given to us as a gift from above to take care and be there every step of the way for our precious little girl.

My children made signs to hang around her basin. Every little while, I'd get prizes and books to send home to my kids from the life support team. I would say it's from Shalva and that she loves them and can't wait to meet her siblings.

At this point we were scheduling a debulking surgery. What is debulking surgery? They are going to debulk the mass by making an incision and opening her up. The goal is to try to get out as much as they can, depending on how much the baby can handle. Then they reconstruct the skin.

As the days were nearing the surgery, I was excited about positive results, but at the same time, very nervous about the procedure and anesthesia. I had some sleepless nights with lots of nerves and worries. I spent lots of time crying and davening.

In the meantime, the children were not taking it well that they couldn't see their baby sister. As time went on, they had more and more questions. They then requested to see her booboo. We then sat down together and spoke about it. I gave them a heads up that I can show it to them, but if they don't feel like they can handle it, that's okay! I started off by showing them some pictures of Shalva's booboo after the Sclerotherapy treatment, when it didn't look as bad, and over the next few days, I continued showing them images. They felt so bad for her. They kissed and rubbed her booboo over the phone. This was as close and as real as it was for them. However, I didn't show them any of the pictures from before any interventions were done.

The day was July 1st. We left the house early in the morning when it was still dark outside. I couldn't utter a word out of my mouth the entire long one hour and twenty-minute journey to the hospital. I was sitting silently, breathing. and in an undertone, saying Tehillim. My husband was nervous, but he also felt excited. He couldn't wait for Shalva's mass to go down in size.

As we arrived in the hospital, I was holding Shalva on my lap I sang, spoke to her, and davened for her. I felt so scared and helpless. I couldn't fathom the idea that my daughter was going through all this pain and hardship. I so badly wanted to just switch places with her. I didn't want her to have to go through any pain and suffering.

The doctors gathered around us, as we all walked down the hallway toward the elevators to go down to the Operating room. I was holding Shalva's hand and we felt as though we were walking on thin air. The nerves came piling in. We gave her a bracha and said some Tehillim. Then, they took Shalva into the OR and escorted us out.

She went in for surgery. I was just sobbing and saying Tehillim the entire time. When the surgery was over, we were informed that the surgery was successful. It seemed like it all went well. I remember the surgeons telling me, "Mom, it was a great success, it looks beautiful, though you're not going to be happy with the way it looks." I was confused and asked why? What was wrong? They said they left some extra skin. This way, if it grows again, it gives her skin room to grow without stretching it. They added that it's an easy fix up for later on.

They debulked and reconstructed about 90% of the outer part of the abdominal wall. With our consent, they saved a piece of tissue for testing and research purposes!

They then discussed with both of us and encouraged us to do a full DNA genetic test to see if there was anything within our DNA or genes that would match the lymphatic malformation. We thought it out, discussed it, and agreed to do it. Results take a few months to come through, so they wanted to do it right away.

Sitting by Shalva's side was a very emotional experience. Seeing her attached to oxygen and attached to fluids was very frightening. They kept her sleeping for a few more hours as she was in lots of pain.

When she woke up, she was given pain meds around the clock, which was very alarming to me. I didn't want her to get immune to it, and I feared what the long-term effects would be with all the prescribed pain medications. They had to wean her off slowly according to the protocol. During the days of and after the surgery, I couldn't hold her as she was very weak, delicate, and sore.

They didn't want anything to touch the area of the incision other than the dressing that they wrapped around her.

The days after the surgery, her swelling decreased, and she was able to fit into a size four diaper. She probably could've gone to a size three, but we didn't want any pressure on her, and therefore kept it loose.

Seeing her progress and reflecting my thoughts back to the pregnancy when they were constantly trying to convince me to terminate, I looked at Shalva and teared up in joy. I was so happy that termination wasn't even an option for me. I asked my husband, "Can you imagine the doctors trying to convince us to abort this beautiful princess?"

We were in the NICU for a while during the stay. We met many people from all different cultures and backgrounds. Unfortunately, it takes such circumstances to really learn to appreciate everyone regardless of their background, culture, or religion. We all had our own story, and the unity was special. There were some other parents that we'd share our story with, and they'd share theirs. The more I heard their stories, the more I was really able to appreciate and thank Hashem for ours. They felt the same way, and they'd tell me, "I don't know how you're going through this, how you're coping, how you have a smile on your face." I realized Hashem really gives each individual what they can handle.

After speaking with some parents, we heard some of their doctors were very negative and encouraged abortion. These courageous women stood up for themselves. Some doctors are quick to offer abortion, and it's unfortunate that with ignorance, the parents go along with it.

As knowledgeable as doctors are, they are not G-D and can't predict the future. There are many stories of parents being told a diagnosis for a baby during pregnancy, and the baby was born 100% healthy. We realized if the parents were more knowledgeable and confident to stand up for themselves and the doctors wouldn't be so quick to terminate, there would be a lot more beautiful, healthy children in the world.

Abortion is a decision that you have to live with for the rest of your life. Before making such a life and death decision, it's important to consult with a Rabbi, a spiritual leader, a mentor, and/or a professional that can help guide you with a clear view. Perhaps can explore other options together.

Over a Shabbos that we spent in the hospital we sat down in the Bikur Cholim room to eat our seudah, and another couple joined us. We got to speak and share our stories with each other. We were discussing how on the outside, no one knows what's going on. When you see someone walking down the street, you don't know what's going on in their personal life.

I can't remember who said this, but it was very powerful. We all know that there are people with health issues. It's going to happen, though we never thought that it would happen to us. It's as though there's a blacklist of people that will have unhealthy children. And now that we're all sitting here in the hospital with our own stories, we came to the realization that there's no blacklist. This can happen to the best of us! We have to just be grateful and thank Hashem for everything we have and really appreciate our health. It's so easy to take our health for granted. Oftentimes we don't even think about our health. It's through these situations that we recognize and appreciate our health and every functional organ in our bodies.

Walking down the street and giving a smile over to people you see, can really make their day! We don't know how much pain they're in or what they're going through in their personal lives. A small smile can make and enlighten someone's day!

In the meantime, Shalva was being monitored, and the children were asking what was taking forever for her to come home every day. I'd ask the doctors and surgeons for updates and plans. They kept saying they were taking it day by day, one day at a time.

At this point I showed my children the pictures of her booboo from birth. They got so emotional and had lots of questions. It was not easy for them to get a grasp on the situation, especially since they were very innocent and young. I made sure to always have my children feel comfortable and safe to ask any questions they may have.

We discussed how Hashem makes everyone different and that everyone has different types of challenges and issues. They were actively involved in the conversation. I continued to tell them that we don't know why we are faced with the challenges we are put through, though I reassured them that G-D is Perfect, and He knows best! If this is the challenge we are faced with, we will embrace it and strengthen ourselves from this! I explained to them that in order for each of us to reach our fullest potential, this is what Hashem gave us to go through. There's no coincidence with anything that happens along the way. What seems to be a sharp bump or slippery road, is in fact exactly what we need to overcome in order for us to reach our greatness and fullest potential. What doesn't break us makes us stronger!

The surgery went well, and Shalva was recovering nicely. They decided to schedule another round of Sclerotherapy procedure. It was scheduled for July 16th.

We want the kids to be as least worried as possible. We would therefore tell the children the night before the procedures, so they didn't have too much time to think and worry about Shalva. When we'd tell them, we'd sit down with them very calmly and let everyone ask all their questions and share their concerns and feelings. I'd listen and validate them and let them know that their worries and feelings are normal and healthy. I'd then reassure them that this is the best thing for Shalva. it's to help her feel better, and this is part of the process to get rid of the booboo. I reminded them Hashem is the ultimate Doctor, and we will daven that Shalva will be healthy and well!

CHAPTER: 10

The night before the procedure, my mother slept over to be with my children, and we stayed in a hotel to be closer to the hospital. Before we went to the hospital, I remember we passed by the 9/11 memorial. We didn't have much time but decided it was worth it to walk by. We saw how many lives were lost and how many families were suffering with the losses. We were heartbroken and sad and remembered that no one has it easy!

Everyone has some sort of challenge, pain or suffering, and it's beyond anyone's understanding. Though it all comes down to the fact that we are in Galus (exile). We all go through some sort of difficulty, hardship, pain, and struggle. We all have our own unique ways of dealing with and going through them. Though it all boils down to perspective, it's very hard. If you can stand up to what you're facing and look at it as a challenge, you'll take whatever it is to overcome it. With your enthusiasm, you'll get through it. It's not easy! The more effort and the harder it is to achieve something, the more accomplished and good you'll feel about yourself.

We continued on to the hospital to go to Shalva. At this point, Shalva was already five weeks and five days old. She was getting bigger and more alert. Being that this was the case, my heart was in shambles knowing that she really was suffering. We all walked her to the Operating Room. As I departed, the nurse gave me a big hug when she saw my heartbroken face.

Before, during, and after every procedure, I was very emotional. However, this time, it was a lot harder for me. I think the other times it was very emotional and hard but being that I was still recovering from giving birth, I was a little out of it. Now I felt back to myself.

Shalva is my princess, my shining star, my beautiful daughter, and she was suffering so much. It's a mother's worst nightmare to see their child in pain. I cried and cried. I stayed with her for the next 24 hours. My husband tried comforting me and took me out. I couldn't enjoy myself as I was just thinking about Shalva!

They continued the Sclerotherapy treatment for the next two days. I saw how Shalva was progressing and that was very reassuring to me. I spent lots of time with her, enjoying every moment of being in her presence.

During this stay, lots of doctors and nurses who weren't Shalva's caregivers came around to see her lymphatic malformation! Since it's so uncommon, it was a great learning experience for all of them to see what such a thing looks like.

Baruch Hashem! Shalva is a healthy child with a big booboo! Everyone adores her as she's a beautiful holy princess. Her face shines, and she's filled with chein (grace).

As I spoke to the doctors to see what the plans are moving forward, they told me they're keeping her monitored, going to do more imaging, and they'll decide after. I then jumped to ask when can we be discharged? This was our daily conversation. As soon as the surgeons would come to check on Shalva, they'd say, "Mom, I know you want to go home but not just yet."

On Monday, the doctors came in and said we were going to do a few more tests and imaging. If everything looks good, you will be discharged as early as Wednesday afternoon!

That was such exciting news. I couldn't wait! I was davening that Shalva should be healthy and well and everything should be good with her so that we could go home together. On Tuesday, when I was speaking to the teams, they said as long as nothing comes up, it's looking good with Shalva, and she'd be able to go home tomorrow!

I quickly called my husband to tell him the most amazing news, that tomorrow was the day we were all waiting for. It's confirmed, we're being discharged tomorrow. We were so grateful to Hashem and decided not to tell anyone. We didn't want any Ayin Hara.

In the meantime, I was a bit worried about whether I'd know how to properly take care of her. The doctors and nurses reassured me that Shalva would be in good hands at home with me, and they gave me lots of very clear instructions on the position she should be in. Not to put pressure on her stomach, keep her in loose clothing, etc. They suggested having an aid come to our house once a week just to check up on Shalva.

The big day arrived. We woke up bright and early and gathered Shalva's car seat and some of her things. We sent our kids off to day camp and headed straight to the hospital. We arranged that my friend would be at my house to watch my kids, and my brother-in-law would drive my toddler home.

Excited and happy, we went in with the car seat straight up to the NICU to Shalva. The nurses greeted us with a big smile and told us it was happening. Shalva will be going home today! I felt so emotional, and I asked them to start gathering the discharge papers and documents I needed to sign. This way, as soon as we have the go ahead, nothing will delay the process.

We thanked all the doctors, surgeons, nurses, and all the hospital staff for everything they did for us! We were in the hospital for six weeks and six days. It's not a place anyone wants to be.

We were so grateful that all the doctors and nurses gave us such warm hospitality and had great bedside manners. We were privileged to be under such good care.

We said our goodbyes to other NICU parents and other friends we've made in the hospital. As I was saying goodbye to one of my friends that I made from another culture, she shared her curiosity and asked me what the fringes are that my husband wears. That's when my husband sat down with her to answer lots of the questions she had regarding Judaism! We kept in touch for a couple of years. As soon as the doctors gave us the okay we hugged and thanked them all, took some pictures, and headed out to the car. This was Shalva's first time seeing sunlight, being outside, and getting fresh air.

Tov L'hodos L'Hashem (it's good to give Thanks To Hashem)! We were so grateful and thankful that we were experiencing this moment in reality. It was our dream to take a healthy princess home, and Baruch Hashem, our dream came true.

The ride home seemed like forever, as we were so excited and antsy. We couldn't wait for our other children to meet her. We knew this would be the best surprise ever.

When we got home, my friend was there watching my oldest daughter. We rang the bell, and as we walked in, my daughter's face looked excited and in shock and asked if this this Shalva. We told her yes, and she was glowing with joy. She started jumping up and down singing and wanted to hold her. She ran to wash up with soap and water. The bell rang, our brother-in-law came to drop off our toddler. My toddler was so excited that he was a big brother that he quickly ran to wash up and see Shalva. A few minutes later, when our two other sons came home, they rang the bell, and as they saw my husband by the door, they were so excited and asked how come you're not at work. Until they took a few steps into the house, and they couldn't believe their eyes. They ran and hugged me. Then quickly washed up. They all wanted to hold their new baby sister. I explained to them that they cannot hold her as she is very delicate, though they could touch her gently and they can all give her kisses.

This was a moment we all cherished and will never forget. This was the day that we were all davening and longing for, and it was real!

We then told our parents and families the good news. Everyone was ecstatic, excited, and happy. That night, my sister-in-law sent over yummy, delicious homemade cookies. I was not up for visitors as I just wanted to give my children the full attention that they deserved, and allow them to get to know Shalva and just take it all in.

I was nervous to go up and down steps with her, so we set up a bedroom on the main floor with a crib for her and a bed. I'd keep an eye on her 24/7.

Bright and early the next morning, my mother came over to visit Shalva. There were a few nights she stayed over to let me sleep through the night. It was a massive help, and I'm really grateful for that.

Being that I was back and forth in the hospital and home every single day, I never had time to properly heal or rest up. I was always coming, going, and doing things. We realized that originally, we didn't want to plan the C-section until after Shavuos. We realized Hashem wanted it to be beforehand and to give me four days to rest.

We had an aid come to our house weekly, just to do some vitals, weigh Shalva, and she'd measure the mass to keep track of it so we would know if it grew. I made lots of visits to my pediatrician often with all of my concerns. Even though the pediatrician never had such a case, they treated us and Shalva as a VIP patient.

We had to have follow-up visits once every other month after the first follow-up visit, with all the surgeons and doctors present. I asked how long we were going to continue with these follow ups. They said we were going to be family for the next three to five years. A very warm, friendly way to say that we would continue with frequent visits for the next couple of years. As time moved on, Baruch Hashem Shalva was progressing, and we were able to come in once every three months.

Since she was born, I wanted to get her earrings, but being that she was in the hospital the first forty-eight days of her life we couldn't do it then. Before going into the OR, or getting an MRI, all jewelry would have to be removed.

And when we got home, I didn't know if and when we'd be having more procedures. I therefore held off with the earrings for a bit.

As a few months passed and Shalva started rolling over and swarming and pushing her body to mobile herself around. I was so excited for my baby. They predicted the worst, and here she was able to move and do what she was supposed to do.

As time moved on, I couldn't believe my eyes. Was that right? Do I see correctly? Hodu LaHashem Ki Tov Ki Lolom Chasdo! My princess is crawling. As tears rolled down my cheeks, I was so joyful and thankful to Hashem. Shalva was reaching all her milestones, and not only that, but it was also within the appropriate time frame of age.

Every time she rolled over, crawled, and got around on her own, I'd think this was the baby that they had no hope with. They wanted to get rid of such a beautiful, healthy precious gem's life.

When she was about nine months old, we decided it was time to get her earrings. She was blossoming so beautifully; it would just enhance her face. We went to get her earrings, and it lit up her face. We showed her pictures of herself with the earrings and let her see them in the mirror. As she looked at it, her face lit up. It was clear she felt like a beautiful princess.

A couple of weeks later, COVID-19 hit home, and the lockdowns began. We were so happy we got to pierce her ears beforehand.

In March 2020, a week after Purim (a Jewish holiday), I got the coronavirus. I was sick, weak, and bed-bound, though I was still nursing. I was concerned and nervous for her to catch the virus.

I called the surgeons and told them that I was sick with COVID-19. I asked if it was life threatening or dangerous for Shalva and how I should go about taking care of her while I was sick. They reassured me that she is not more high risk than any other child. I can continue nursing her as much as possible.

I should try not to breathe on her, keep myself very sanitary, and not kiss her. They said if she had a fever or any other symptoms, I should call them right away. Baruch Hashem, after a couple of days, I felt better, and Shalva and the rest of my family stayed healthy. No one caught any of the symptoms.

I was informed that due to COVID-19, the visits will begin taking place virtually and only to come in person for absolute emergencies. The convenience of having the appointments virtually was amazing, though it wasn't the same. We missed being seen in person.

During the year, they were discussing doing some intervention near the kidneys, and we'd go to a center every three months to get imaging done. They were hoping to schedule for the summertime, though as the COVID-19 pandemic arose and the hospitals were getting stricter, they were only doing emergency procedures. The schedule kept getting postponed. They just kept her monitored through the imaging.

Back when we were in the hospital, we noticed that Shalva's second toe was a bit bigger than her big toe. When we mentioned that to the doctors, they said it was an overgrowth and we should be seen by an orthopedic surgeon sometime after discharge.

Our team of doctors recommended an orthopedic surgeon to see Shalva and we scheduled an appointment. Nervous as to what we were going to be told, we kept on reminding each other that everything is in Hashem's hands.

The day arrived, and we met with the doctor. After he looked at her toe and did some X-rays, he spoke with us and told us that the best option would be is to amputate the toe. As keeping the toe can affect her ability to walk and cause her to lose balance easily. She'd have a hard time fitting into shoes and it can get in the way of her life.

I then asked him what he would do if this was his child. He said he'd talk it over with his wife and discuss the pros and cons. He would amputate the toe without a sliver of doubt to give her the best opportunities in life, and he wouldn't want her toe to get in the way of life. He'd definitely amputate it if his wife was on board.

Right then, my husband felt he got clarity. He didn't want this to affect her childhood, future, or her walking and balance. He asked if we could schedule a surgery for amputation. The doctor said the younger she is, the better it will heal. The toes will collide next to each other so that there won't be a gap between the toes. So, unless you're counting it, it wouldn't be noticeable that she has a missing toe.

I was very uncomfortable about this and asked if there was any way to shave down the skin or any other option. Once we amputate it there's no getting the toe back. It's a done deal. I was also concerned for her emotionally. I didn't want her to feel different than everyone else. I didn't want her to feel like the odd one out with having nine toes. He understood my feelings and recommended that we schedule the surgery, think about it, and discuss it. Worst case scenario, if I decide I don't want to proceed, we can cancel the surgery before the date it was scheduled for. I was not happy about it, yet I agreed to those terms. We got all the documents and papers and headed out.

CHAPTER: 11

The whole car ride home, my husband and I were discussing it. He very strongly felt that amputating the toe would be the best thing for her. He said as long as it's okay with halacha (Jewish law), this is what we're doing, he said he'd ask his Rabbi.

I broke out in tears and said we're not talking about cutting her nails or her hair. It'll never grow back. Once it's amputated, it'll be gone forever. I couldn't fathom that we were making such a big life decision for her that we could never take back.

I suggested maybe let's wait until she's older and see how she feels about it. Being that it's her body, it's something she'll have to live with or without for the rest of her life. He was opposed to that, and felt she'd be happiest and have a much better life without this toe.

We got home, my husband spoke to his Rabbi, and he said in this situation, a toe amputation is permissible. My husband was very excited to tell me. He felt he had such a sense of clarity. I was very emotional about this decision. However, I definitely didn't want the responsibility of making a bad decision for my child on my shoulders, so I gave the okay.

Once I gave him the okay, it was not sitting right with me. I was super emotional, had a loss of appetite, and couldn't sleep at night. Something very strong in me was saying not to do it. I discussed it with my husband, and he understood my feelings. I made it very clear I'm not having her toe amputated without going for a second opinion.

It was 2 days before the surgery was scheduled, and I called to cancel. I hung up the phone, feeling such a relief. I felt a heavy burden off my shoulders, and I could think straight. I immediately called up an organization to refer me to an orthopedic surgeon within my insurance plan. After I told them the whole situation, they gave me a referral. I thanked them and right away made the call.

I called the office to make an appointment. I was straight up and honest with them. I let them know the whole story and that I was using them as a second opinion. The secretary seemed pleasant over the phone and scheduled an appointment.

The day arrived, and we came to this orthopedic appointment. The doctor saw all the images and took some more. He explained that amputation is a very aggressive approach and that sometimes it is needed, though that would be a last resort. He recommended to try other alternatives in the meantime.

He suggested stunting the growth. Before doing that, he wanted the toe to grow a bit more, so that by the time her feet and toes develop, this toe would fit in and be proportionate with her other toes. I was very happy with this appointment and was looking forward to going ahead with this. I felt so grateful that I didn't jump into the amputation of the toe. He said we should come back in nine months for a follow up to see how the toe is growing.

He offered to have an Orthotist measure Shalva's foot and get her custom-made shoes. This way, by the time she's walking, she'll have shoes that she can wear. It takes a few months for insurance to approve and have it ready to be picked up, so we did that.

On the way home, we discussed this option that the doctor mentioned, and we both felt satisfied and happy with it. I was so happy we were all on the same page and agreed to this. I was so grateful that I went for this second opinion.

In the meantime, Shalva was growing, and she started standing and shortly after, started walking holding on. This milestone broke me into tears of joy and happiness. With every milestone she reached, we felt so blessed to experience miracles in front of our very own eyes. It was always very emotional, and we felt and had tremendous gratitude towards Hashem.

We continued with the virtual follow ups with the other doctors and surgeons and Baruch Hashem, everything was going well with Shalva's LM (lymphatic malformation). Now that the hospitals were calming down and the pandemic restrictions were being waived, we were discussing surgery by the kidneys.

The nine months since our appointment for a second opinion flew by and it was time for our follow up. We came back to the appointment and updated the doctor with Shalva's milestone that she started walking. They checked her toe out, then they took her for more X-rays and spoke to us. This time, with the look on his face, I knew something was up. I asked what's going on? He said very softly and with lots of compassion that in the past, we discussed stunting the growth. Though at the rate it was growing, it seemed like that wouldn't be an ideal option any longer. It's not the skin that's the problem, It's the actual bone under the toe that is growing at a really rapid pace.

He must've seen the look on my face when he reassured me that he really wished there was something to do to save the toe. He said at this point if we stunt the growth, at a later time the toe will have to be amputated. If you decide to go with that route, it means many procedures. Plus, later on in her teenage years, when she'd have to amputate the toe, she would have to be in a cast for six weeks followed by a boot for a couple of months. She would be missing out on lots of school, social events, etc. That's the smaller part of the issue. The bigger problem was that there would be a massive gap on her foot between the big toe to the middle toe. To fix that there would have to be a lot more intervention.

He said we should think about it, and if we are focused on the bigger picture and what's best for her, it would, unfortunately, be ideal for her toe to be amputated as soon as possible. We heard him out and understood that there was no way out of it. We realized that this was going to happen. Her toe would be amputated.

We thanked him for his sensitivity and headed out. On the way back we discussed how we appreciated his honesty, and we were super impressed with his bedside manner and the way he explained everything to us. I told my husband; I was still happy we went for a second opinion and didn't regret canceling the surgery the first time around. I felt we did our hishtadlus, and at this point, it's in Hashem's hands. All we can do is daven. I was emotional that this was the reality, though I accepted it with love from above. My husband was very happy, because since the first time it was mentioned, he felt this was ideal.

Being that we decided to go ahead with the toe amputation, we discussed whether we should go ahead with the first doctor or the second. We decided to have a follow up with the original orthopedic surgeon we met, and we will make a decision from there. We then scheduled an appointment.

The day of the appointment arrived, and we woke up with all different thoughts and feelings going through our minds. As we were driving on the highway, we were speaking, and my husband said he feels 100% confident that this doctor is the one we will use. We both agreed that the best option was to be honest and tell him about our second opinion.

We got to the doctor and waited nervously in the waiting room. We were hoping he wouldn't take offense to the fact we went elsewhere and didn't keep him updated until we were about to see him. As they called Shalva's name, we quickly got up and went to the room.

The doctor walked in, and my husband started telling him everything and I added in. He was glad and supportive that we went for another opinion, and we felt more confident about the situation. He said it's very important to be fully on board before committing to such a procedure. He had some more X- rays done to see what it looked like. When he compared it to the previous images, he saw a tremendous growth.

At that moment, my husband felt that this doctor would be the best shaliach (messenger) from Hashem to do this procedure for Shalva. He was very knowledgeable, confident, respectful, thought-out, and experienced. I apologized for canceling at the last minute, though he was super understanding and glad we were doing it then.

Everything in life that is supposed to happen, happens at the very exact moment it needs to. Ten months prior to this appointment, it was not the right time, and it could've held her back from some of her milestones. Now that she had reached lots of milestones and was running around all over the place, it was a good time to do it. The doctor told us it can cause some regression with her walking, though she'll get right back to it with time.

He gave us lots of time to explain everything and answered all our questions. He made sure I felt confident, and that I was really ready for this. He didn't want me to feel forced into making such a big decision. He wanted it to come from me wholeheartedly and to make sure I was sincerely on board. I said I will just daven and hoped that this would be the best thing for Shalva. I know Hashem is guiding me, so I will follow in His lead.

I told him I appreciated all the time he gave talking and explaining everything to us. As well as his understanding, honesty, and sensitivity. I then said I'm ready to schedule a procedure. I signed the documents, and he gave us instructions and papers to take home. With that, we thanked him and left.

On the way home, I took a few moments to daven to Hashem that we had made the right move and that this doctor should be the perfect messenger to amputate Shalva's toe without any complications. It should heal fast, healthy and easily, as Shalva had been through so much in her little life. I didn't want her to suffer any longer.

We spoke about the appointment, and we both felt satisfied. I felt satisfied, but was very nervous, and decided I was not going to think too much about it. The more I thought of it, the more frightened I'd be. My husband felt that this toe would give her a lot of problems throughout life. He felt she'd be a much happier child and have a better life without it. He didn't want the toe to get in the way of her life.

CHAPTER: 12

In the meantime, my husband spoke to his Rabbi, and he thought it would be good for us and our children to move to New Jersey. My husband spoke to me about it, I had my concerns and reservations about it. I said if this is the guidance you got from your Rabbi, let's do it.

It was mid-June when we started to look into moving to New Jersey. We were going back and forth from New York to New Jersey to look at houses and to find schools for our children. We applied to many schools and had a hard time finding a school that would even interview our older daughter. They were all full and were not accepting new applicants. We didn't give up and kept looking until we found schools that were open to meeting us.

We devoted one day for the boys to be interviewed in a few different schools. The meetings were back-to-back and went well. Baruch Hashem, we got my boys into school right away.

It was a month before the school year began, and we still hadn't found a school for my daughter or four-year-old son. We also hadn't found a house to buy or rent.

We already told the landlord that we were moving as of the end of July. We told the schools that our kids were currently in that we will not be attending for the following school year. We also signed the contract for the boy's new school.

I was starting to doubt if this was a smart decision. What will we do if we don't have a place to live and don't have a school for two of our children. My husband kept on reassuring me not to worry and that it would all work out.

In the meantime, we had a follow up for Shalva. They did an ultrasound and checked on the lymphatic malformation near the kidneys. To their surprise, it was no longer there. The doctors were confused and had no idea how these images contradicted previous imaging. They said it must've been good luck. We understand that nothing happens coincidentally or by chance. It all comes from Hashem! And we, along with many others daven for Shalva on a daily basis. We have no power; everything is destined by Hashem. The only power we have is with our tefillos (prayers), and that is a real superpower. No Tefillah goes unanswered. We sometimes don't understand the answer, and sometimes we need to wait as it's not the right time. Sometimes the answer is no, and that Hashem knows what's best! The more concentration and the more effort and energy one puts into their prayers the more powerful it becomes. We had no doubt that Hashem answered our tefillos and we just witnessed a great miracle. We were forever so grateful to Hashem. We were all so ecstatic and happy. Thank you, Hashem!

At this point, I was a few weeks into a new pregnancy and felt very weak, dizzy, and nauseous. Between packing and looking for homes and schools, there was a lot going on. However, it definitely was a great distraction from Shalva's toe amputation procedure that was coming up.

CHAPTER: 13

I t was the last week of July, and Baruch Hashem, we found a temporary six-month rental. We decided to take it. We thought it would be the perfect amount of time for us to settle in and to continue looking to buy a house. The rental would be available in about three weeks. We signed the contract and felt that things were slowly and surely falling into place.

The night before the procedure my sister-in-law and friend came over to help me finish packing up the house. In the meantime, my kids stayed in my parents' house, and we stayed with Shalva at my sister in law's house.

It was the night before the procedure was scheduled. I was very nervous and wanted to go to sleep early as I knew we had to be on the road by 4:00 a.m. I tried to sleep, but between my nerves, emotions, and everything going on in my life, I had a very difficult time.

I finally fell asleep at about 1:00 a.m., and the alarm woke us up at 3:30. I woke up feeling very weak, dizzy, and nauseous with morning sickness. I had no choice but to ignore my body's symptoms and go. We quickly jumped out of bed, got ready in a hurry, and hit the road.

During the entire drive towards the hospital, I was weak and nauseous. I was vomiting from morning sickness, and my nerves and worries were not helping the situation. I was taking deep breaths while my husband was trying to soothe and relax me. He kept telling me that this was the best thing for Shalva. When she grows up, she'll be forever grateful, Hashem is the ultimate Doctor, and everything will be alright.

We got to the hospital. Being that it was during the COVID pandemic, we had to wear masks. I held Shalva in my arms, opened my Tehillim, and started reciting it. I didn't get too far, as my nausea was extreme. My husband held her the rest of the time that we were in the triage as I couldn't stop vomiting. It was a mixture of nerves and morning sickness. In the meantime, my husband was learning his Daf Yomi (daily page of the Talmud).

After they checked all her vitals, the surgeon and anesthesiologist came to explain everything. We signed the consent forms, and they asked us if we had any questions or concerns. At that point, we told the doctor that we had spoken with our Rabbi, and we needed the toe back for proper burial. In our Jewish custom, we don't dispose of any organ or limb. The doctor was very understanding, and he seemed to be familiar with that concept. He got us a consent form to sign, and he said after the surgery is over, the toe will be given to the Pathology department for some testing. Only the ones who are burying it can be the ones to pick it up. He gave us the contact number to be in touch and said we should wait a couple of days. During this conversation, I had shivers down my spine. It was very emotional.

It was time, and they came to pick Shalva up to take her to the OR. We weren't allowed to walk her to the OR, so I gave her a huge hug and kiss. I told her I'll daven for her, and Hashem is going to be guiding the doctor every step of the way. I said a prayer as I held her hand, gave her another hug and kiss, and off they went to the OR.

We were told to take all our belongings and wait in the waiting area, so that's what we did. My husband continued learning his daf (page of the Talmud). Even though I spent most of the time vomiting, any moment I had, I utilized it for davening. It was the most awful, unpleasant feeling. In general, when I wear masks, I feel very uncomfortable and claustrophobic. Being that I was sick with morning sickness and vomiting, it felt so much worse.

A little while later, the doctor met us and told us the surgery was a great success, everything worked out beautifully. The toe is being sent to the pathology department, and Shalva will have to be in a cast for about three months. Following that she'll have to wear a special shoe for six to nine months. He said to keep Shalva off her feet for twenty-four hours. After that, when she feels ready, she can stand and walk.

I was so happy it was over and done with, and it all worked out well without any complications. We were very grateful to Hashem. I felt emotionally drained, and my body was so weak. My husband felt so much happiness as he knew Shalva would have a great life without the toe getting in her way.

She was in the recovery room for a little while until she woke up and drank some apple juice and had some ice. After they saw she was eating and able to hold her food down, they discharged us.

Originally, our plan was to go straight to my parents' house to be with our children. Being that I was so weak emotionally and physically, we went straight to where we were staying, and I went straight to bed with Shalva. I had no energy to talk to anyone. We took a little nap, and my husband went to our other children. By the time he came back at 8:30 p.m., I was already out for the night. Shalva woke up in pain once throughout the night. I gave her some Motrin and water, then she slept until the morning.

In the morning when we woke up, she wanted to get out of bed. I explained to her that she couldn't walk or stand, she was not happy about that. I showed her the cast and explained to her with great sensitivity to her understanding as to why she was in a cast. I showed her the special boot shoe the doctor gave her to wear over the cast, and she was excited about that.

She had a hard time sitting in one place, she wanted her independence and freedom back. She wanted to be able to walk and get around on her own. In terms of pain, she was great. She was a real trooper during the day, and she didn't need any Tylenol or Motrin. The nights were more challenging. We gave her Tylenol and Motrin for the first three nights, and after that, she wasn't in pain anymore. She was running around and playing as if nothing ever happened to her.

I was so happy to see her standing and walking and was so thankful that she didn't regress, as was expected. I was so happy to know this was behind us.

About a week after the surgery, we contacted the pathology team to see when the toe could be picked up. They told us the address of where it could be picked up from. It had to be the one burying it or the organization that buries that can pick it up.

My family knew someone involved in Chevra Kadisha, which is an organization of people that prepares the deceased for proper burial in accordance with Jewish law. They gave me the contact number. I was about to call, but I just couldn't get myself to do that. It was really frightening and scary. I quickly called my husband and told him that I could not be the one calling, dealing, or arranging anything with the Chevra Kadisha. It was too scary and nerve wracking.

My husband understood and took that responsibility on his shoulders. He made the call, gave them all the information they needed, and made the payment. My husband called to follow up to make sure they picked up the toe. Then they told him when they were planning to bury it. He called to follow up to make sure it was buried, and that everything worked out.

Dealing with Chevra Kadisha and burials is very emotionally heartbreaking. We were shaken up inside. It was a great big wakeup call and a real eye opener for us to be thankful for every little and big part of our body. We became sensitive and realized how every small limb and organ in a person's body is so precious. Unfortunately, we tend to take them for granted. It's the times when we don't have it anymore that we realize how beautiful, important, and special every organ and limb that Hashem gifted us with really is, and what we would do to save a small bone. We were so grateful that we were only having her toe buried, and she is as full of life as possible, Baruch Hashem!

A couple of days after the surgery, my husband's sister hosted us for the weekend in upstate New York. When we packed out on Sunday, we headed straight to New Jersey as it was our big day of officially moving into our new rental home. It was a long three-and-a-half-hour ride after a long and emotionally overwhelming week. We got to the house, and all our luggage was everywhere. It was a huge job to settle in.

My husband took the kids out for supper to a pizza store. I started preparing everyone's beds and unpacking some clothing so we could start off the week functionally. I tried to do as much as I could, as I knew that I had no extra help. As of the next morning, my husband would be commuting back and forth every day to work.

Weak, tired and drained, I pushed myself to my limits and got the bedrooms prepared. My husband also did a small shopping to stock up the house with basic essentials and necessities. That was a massive help for me.

The next day, our new life started. My husband left the house to start his commute bright and early before any of us were awake. My kids were all home with me, and we had unpacked luggage and boxes everywhere. There was not much space to maneuver around inside, though we had a nice, big, spacious backyard that the kids spent lots of time playing in. They got to meet some neighbors and made some friends. I was just trying to unpack whilst taking extra care of Shalva and tending to all of my children's needs.

By the time my husband would be done work and get home, all the kids were already sound asleep for the night. My husband was always a very hands-on father and helped out a lot and played with the kids. This was a very hard change for my children to get used to the fact they barely get to see him.

Mid-week, the kids started school. It was the first day and they had a half day of school without school transportation. I felt stuck in limbo; I didn't know what to do. I was a pretty new driver and didn't feel comfortable driving on these roads. I came from city driving, with a traffic light at every corner and a speed limit of up to 25 mph, to living in New Jersey with lots of highways, intersections, and an average speed limit of 40/50 mph. I didn't feel comfortable driving without my husband practicing driving with me first. Being that he was barely around, there was no time for practicing.

On the first day of school, I had a few options. I could take an Uber with the whole family in the car, which the thought of was too overwhelming for me. The boys could miss their first day, though that wasn't practical or realistic. Or I can walk them to school, which was a forty-five-minute walk in the heat. I thought about it, packed everyone with water bottles and snacks, and decided we were going to take this journey and walk.

I wheeled Shalva in the carriage and had my other children walk. At first, they were excited about going on this mission. As we continued walking with the sun beaming on us and with lots of humidity, the children kept on saying are we there yet, how much longer, etc. We took some breaks, and they drank some water. We enjoyed the scenery and there were some hills that the kids challenged themselves to run up. There were some streets that were very scary to walk on as there were no sidewalks. They all finished their water bottles, and we got to talk about their feelings about starting a new school. They were really excited and nervous. I reassured them that it was such a healthy and normal feeling.

We finally got to the corner of the block, where there were no traffic lights, and a big highway to cross over. It took about ten minutes of us waiting until cars stopped to let us cross over. We finally arrived. I walked them up the flight of stairs as they were huffing and puffing, sweaty, and their faces were beat red like a tomato. I washed their faces and gave them more water, wished them blessings, and hugged and kissed them goodbye.

The school gave me the phone number of a parent of one of the boys from the school who lives about a ten-minute walk from us so we can try to arrange rides with them.

On the way back, it was Shalva, my older daughter, and my four-year-old son. We got to schmooze (chat) the whole way home, and they loved the attention.

When I got home, I told my family about our morning journey to school, and one of my sisters arranged for her sister-in-law to pick my boys up that afternoon. It was a massive help and I was so grateful. My boys were dropped off, and they had a wonderful start to the new school year.

I didn't have a chance to unpack, so it was very squishy indoors. The kids played out in the backyard as much as possible.

I called a parent from the school that the secretary suggested. She was so sweet and offered to take my kids to and from school every day until transportation began. It worked out amazingly, and it really helped me out. In the morning, we would walk ten minutes to their house and in the afternoon, they'd drop the boys off at our home. The arrangement worked out beautifully.

In the meantime, we still haven't found a school for my nine-year-old daughter or my four-year-old son. We were trying to unpack and settle in whilst making lots of phone calls to many schools. We tried having Rabbis and others help us with their connections, but it was to no success.

This move was a very hard adjustment for all of us in different ways. My boys had to get used to their new schools, and my nine-year-old and four-year-old had a hard time adjusting. Knowing that everyone around them was in school, my daughter was embarrassed to be seen outside without a school uniform. She took it very personally that she had no school to go to. I felt overwhelmed with the whole move, doing everything myself and with Shalva by my side still recovering, it was not an easy transition. It was also really hard for me that my husband was barely around. There were times when I felt like I was at a total loss. Being that I wasn't driving, that made it a lot harder as there was nowhere really to go within walking distance. I felt locked up. This move started turning into a terrible nightmare.

CHAPTER: 14

As days and weeks passed, and we had no updates with schools, I was literally on the phone day and night with many wonderful people trying to help. I started to fall into a real low. I wasn't taking to this well. It was so painful to see my children begging for school, to be like everyone else. I did everything I possibly could to be a good mother and get my children in, though to no success.

I became very emotionally overwhelmed, and it was not a healthy situation. I started to feel really homesick and wanted to move back to my old neighborhood in New York. Lots of resentment started growing within me. I felt really miserable and was pleading with my husband to move back to New York.

He was a lot more optimistic at the time, and he kept on telling me if this is where we are, this is exactly where Hashem wants us to be. There are no mistakes and no coincidences. Hashem is perfect, and He knows best. If this is where He sent us, this is the very place we are supposed to be.

I believe in Hashem and have no doubt that everything that happens is meant to be Not only that, but it's also actually for the best. At the moment, it was very hard to feel, see, and think in this way. I was still able to say this and deep down I knew this. I tried listening to some shiurim (lectures) and reading some books on Emunah (faith) and gratitude. I was just trying to see the light in my darkness.

Thinking back, everything happened way too fast, with not much time to process nor without the proper help. It was definitely very challenging, and I kept telling myself if Hashem put me through it, I believe and I know He will guide me through it. I tried my best to stay positive, though it was not easy.

A little time passed, and it was right around Sukkos (A Jewish holiday) time. My husband was working tirelessly every single day. Two days before Sukkos, he took some time to build our Sukkah. I was inside cooking and baking in preparation for the Yom Tov (holiday).

During the day, I noticed that Shalva's mass looked like it had grown a bit. I told my husband to buy the next size up diapers before Sukkos starts. In the meantime, I called the surgeon's office to schedule a follow up appointment for after the Chag (holiday).

Sukkos began, and we were so excited to finally be together, unite as a family, and have lots of quality time together. The first night of Sukkos was really beautiful. We enjoyed the beautiful weather, sitting in our Sukkah with my husband and boys singing beautifully, and eating a delicious homemade festive meal. It was a beautiful start to the Yom Tov.

The next morning, my husband went to Shul (synagogue) to daven, and I was home with the little children. Shalva woke up, and she didn't look well. I tried feeding her, and she had no appetite. I made sure she drank to keep her hydrated.

I took her outside on a little walk for some fresh air until my husband got back home. I told him to take a look at Shalva. He said she looks pale, let's keep a close eye on her. We ate the meal and tried to enjoy the moments. Shalva was not eating and didn't look good, which made me really concerned. The entire day, we watched her every second. We didn't let her in a room by herself. That night, I put her to bed, said Shema and some Tehillim, and kissed her good night. I was not at ease. I literally came to check in on her every five to ten minutes when I was awake and couldn't sleep. Throughout the night, I checked on her every half hour to an hour.

The next morning, when she woke up, she was a lot more pale and didn't look well, though she was very playful. I was hoping that she would eat, which she did a little. Later on in the day, she looked so weak and frail. We had a hard time closing her diaper as it was getting too tight. The mass was growing. We were very scared and didn't know what to do. We decided to wait until the nighttime, when the first days of Sukkos were over, to contact her surgeon.

My husband took the children to the park, and Shalva stayed home with me. She was sad she couldn't go, so I took her for a walk around the block. She was very white and pale, so I took her back home and fed her whatever she'd eat and gave her lots to drink.

The day went by very slowly and Shalva was looking worse and worse. We tried keeping her distracted and played with her a lot. We read books with her and sang songs to her. As the day was nearing its end, we ate a meal together and tried enjoying the last little bits of the day. Shortly after, my husband went to Shul as I got our kids ready for bed. He came home, and I quickly rushed to get my phone. I took pictures of her mass from all different angles and sent them to the surgeon right away.

We then put everyone to bed, and I put Shalva to sleep in my bed. I didn't want her to be alone and just wanted her at my side. Within forty-five minutes of when I sent the surgeon an email, she called me and said, "Mom, Shalva has to come in to be seen right away." She said we should go straight to the ER, and she's going to send a message over that we're on the way.

I quickly ran to take a shower as my husband called his sister to see if anyone could come to sleep over for the night to watch our kids as we went to the hospital. Right away, she said she'll send two nieces over.

I quickly packed up a few things for both Shalva and I, as I didn't know how long I'd be admitted for. We left in a hurry, nervous as can be. My husband was driving. Due to construction, lots of highways were blocked off, and there was an immense amount of traffic. At one point, we were at a still point in traffic until finally we started to move. My husband got off an exit, which helped us skip lots of traffic.

We finally got to the hospital, and due to COVID, my husband didn't know if they'd let both parents in the hospital. He said he'd look for parking as I checked in with Shalva.

I checked in with Shalva and filled out some paperwork. They asked for my insurance information. Since we just moved from New York to New Jersey, we were off of insurance and in the process of trying to get onto a new one. They said we should make sure to deal with it as soon as possible. In the meantime, there was no service. I had no reception, and my phone wasn't working. My internet was down, so my husband and I had no way of reaching each other.

Finally, at about 5:30 a.m. I noticed a sign that said there was Wi-Fi. I asked the nurse to help me out, and I was finally able to call my husband. He waited in the car all night as he wasn't sure if I'd be admitted or not, and he had no way of reaching me. I told him that he was allowed to come in. So, he came in for a little bit until they were ready to admit us.

He then headed back to our children in the morning. When they woke up, they went to my sister-in-law's house, so my husband met them there. I spoke with him and told him to make sure to give the kids a good, fun day. I want them to enjoy Chol Hamoed (The intermediate days of the holiday). Even though we were in the hospital, I didn't want them to lose out in any way.

I also told him that it's very important to take care of insurance for Shalva as soon as possible. Usually, I deal with this, but being that I was in the hospital, I didn't have the headspace to. I got him the number to an organization that helps with insurance. He quickly called, and they referred him to an agency. He thanked them and hung up the phone.

He quickly called the agency. They emailed us forms that had to be filled out, and they had lots of patience to walk us through the process. We explained our situation, and they quoted us the best out of state coverage insurance plan for Shalva.

He then called me, updated me, and told me he did everything on his end. There were a few things I needed to fill out on the forms. Then he said he was going on an outing with our children, his sister and family to the Popcorn Park Zoo. I was very glad he got to take them on a nice family outing. The kids really enjoyed it and had a great experience.

In the meantime, from the ER through admission, they took some blood work, did some ultrasounds, and testing. They said it seemed that Shalva had an infection, so they gave her antibiotics through IV. They kept her monitored. I arrived at the hospital on Tuesday at about 1:30 a.m., and they kept her there until Friday. They discharged us and sent us home with antibiotics to be taken orally.

My kids were so excited. They came with my husband to pick us up from the hospital. We came home and quickly started preparing for Shabbos. I'm usually not so advanced, but because so much was going on in my life, I decided that when I cook for Sukkos, I will make everything and freeze it so I can enjoy the rest of the holiday. Little did I know Hashem set this up. We had yummy, delicious homemade meals because I already cooked everything. My children all showered and bathed, and we all got ready for Shabbos.

Friday night after the meal, I told my husband that Shalva didn't look right. I was nervous that maybe we should call Hatzalah. My husband said she was just discharged today so let us give it some time and keep an eye out for her. I was nervous, so I just kept davening to Hashem for her to be better.

Throughout the night, I kept her in my bedroom to keep a really close eye on her. Shabbos morning, she woke up looking the same as the night before.

As the day progressed, her looks and behaviors regressed. The mass seemed to be getting bigger. It was a hard Shabbos.

As soon as Shabbos was over, my husband made Havdalah (a ritual ceremony to make a separation between Shabbos and weekdays). Then he put the children to bed as I took more photos of Shalva's mass and sent them to the surgeon. I waited an hour and then two. It was getting late, so we just went to sleep.

The next morning, at around 9 a.m., I got a phone call from the surgeon saying. "Mom, I received the pictures, and it looks like the lymphatic malformation is acting up and angry. Pack up for at least a week and make arrangements for your children as we will have to do some sort of intervention on Shalva." She said that in the future if I send her emails and she doesn't respond right away I should call, not just wait for a response.

I ran to the other room to update my husband. My kids were so happy that we were home and that we would have a family fun day of Chol Hamoed. I felt so bad to tell them. We all gathered around the room together with my husband, and I told them that since Shalva's booboo got bigger, she's not feeling well. I just spoke to her doctor and was told we have to go back to the hospital.

My kids asked if we could first do something fun with the whole family. I apologized to them and said I'd love to, though Shalva really needs to be seen right away. My kids did not take this well. They took it very personally that I was going to the hospital, so I didn't have time to spend the holiday with them. My heart was shattered. I explained to them that this was an emergency. I told them how much I loved them and wished to spend Sukkos together at home with our family.

I then quickly tried calling my parents, but I couldn't get through to them. I tried messaging them and my single siblings, but no one was answering. I got in touch with another sister and asked her to try reaching my parents for me. After about an hour, my mother called me back.

I told her everything and that we would be in the hospital today for sure and possibly until the end of Sukkos. I didn't know for how long. I asked if she could have some of my children over. She said of course, and she can have all of them. I decided to send the three boys to my parents in New York and send my daughter to my sister-in-law who lived locally.

With the arrangements all planned, I quickly put up a load of laundry and had to wait for it to be ready. In the meantime, we started packing whatever we could. My sister-in-law picked up my children and took them to the park while we were packing up to leave.

I finally finished packing and my kids got home. We fed them, my sister-in-law took my daughter, and we all headed to the car. The whole car ride, my boys were really nervous and scared. They wanted to know if Shalva was going to be okay, what's going to happen to her, and what are the doctors going to do. I told them for now, let's daven for her, and when I have updates, I'll let them know.

I didn't want them to be worried, especially that they were not with me. I explained to them that over Chol Hamoed they could be in touch with me. Though when the second days of Sukkos start we can't use electricity of any sort. So, they won't be able to contact me.

They love my parents, though they were not happy about going to them for Yom Tov. They wanted the family to be together. They continued talking, asking questions, and expressing their feelings. I tried my best to reassure them.

CHAPTER: 15

As we were nearing the hospital, I started saying my goodbyes to them. They were sad and started crying. My heart was torn apart. I gave them all big hugs and kisses and told them I'll miss them and how I can't wait to see them and be home with them. On that note, I took Shalva and went into the ER. My husband continued his drive to drop off the boys.

As soon as I left the car, I quickly called my husband up. I told him, being that our kids are really not taking this well, I want him to buy them some presents and take them on an outing. He should spend the day with them until they go to bed, and he meets me back at the hospital.

He then continued on his way with our three boys, and I went into the ER. It was early afternoon as I checked into the hospital. They had us wait a few minutes and shortly after took us into the ER. They did her vitals right away and ordered an ultrasound and blood work for her. They told us they were informed that we were coming and would let the surgeons know we'd arrived.

The nurses came to do blood work, and Shalva was really scared. I lay down, and she snuggled into my arm. I told her she could squeeze my hand as tight as she wanted to. They tried to find a good vein, but they were having a very difficult time. They finally thought they had found the spot, and they tried, though it was not a good bloodline. I tried soothing Shalva as she was crying in pain and fear. A nurse came and turned on the baby shark song to try to distract, but with no success. They tried in both her hands and then went to her feet. They finally got a good vein in the foot. They said they would take a little extra blood in case they need to do additional testing.

I felt so bad for her. Every extra prick was so heartbreaking for me. I shed so many tears with Shalva. They told me to wait for the ultrasounds to come. Hours passed, and we were still waiting for the ultrasounds. They said we would be admitted, and they were waiting for a room to be available.

In the meantime, I fed Shala, and then she took a nap. She woke up a few hours later, and we were still waiting for ultrasounds. It was already nighttime, so I fed her supper. Then I spoke to my husband, and he said he had a great day with the kids, and just got them to bed. He's going to pick up some food for us, and head right on over.

We continued to wait, and within two hours from when I spoke to my husband, he arrived. He came with a gift for Shalva. She was so excited! We opened it up and let her play with her new doll set as we ate supper.

After a long wait, they finally came in to do an ultrasound on Shalva. She was confused about what was happening. I explained to her that they were going to put gel around her tummy and use a special machine that's a camera. The machine would take a picture of the inside of her tummy. We said they needed to see the booboo to see what was going on. I made sure she was comfortable, and she snuggled into me as they did the ultrasound. My husband was making some jokes, telling her we saw everything she ate that day. She found that to be really funny and laughed. She was very cooperative throughout the ultrasound. When it was done, we gave her a treat.

They left the room, and shortly after, some residents came in to speak with us. They told us that after seeing the ultrasounds, the mass definitely grew. The plan was that they put in an order for an MRI for Shalva in the morning, so she won't be able to eat anything past midnight. They said that based on the MRI they will decide how to proceed. We thanked them for the update as they left the room.

A nurse then came in to check her vitals and said that we got a room. We were ready to be admitted, and she led us to our room. I made sure to feed

Shalva more as I wanted to make sure she was completely full, being that it was nearing midnight.

They gave her a crib, and she did not want to go into it. I asked them if we could get her a bed, and they agreed. As long as I'd stay with her every minute. I couldn't leave her alone, and so that's what we did.

After this long, tiring day, we finally went to sleep. It was a disturbed sleep with getting woken up every few hours for vitals. It was Hoshana Rabbah (The seventh day of Sukkos). We woke up at about 8 a.m., and Shalva wanted to eat. I told her the doctors said we couldn't eat yet, and I tried playing with her, reading books, and keeping her occupied.

In the meantime, my husband finished davening and started learning his daf (page of the Talmud) by the table in the room. Being that Shalva was going in for an MRI soon, they wanted to get more blood work, so they did it. At about 9:30 a.m., the surgeons came in to check on her and to see how she was doing. She was extremely pale and didn't look well. They checked her blood results and saw her hemoglobin numbers dropped dangerously low to 4.9.

They were extremely concerned and said she needed to have a blood transfusion right away. They explained to us what it was, along with the risks and benefits and had us sign a consent to agree. It was frightening. I knew it was for her safety, so we agreed.

It was a very frightening moment for all of us. My husband was so engrossed in his learning that he didn't hear or notice anything that was going on in the room. The doctors and nurses all gathered around Shalva and me. They were discussing how to proceed. They then left our bedside for a few minutes to come up with a plan. A few minutes later they came back in and said there was a change of plans. There was no time for an MRI, they were going to have a CAT scan done right away. From there Shalva is going to go directly to the OR area. Based on what they see they'll decide what procedure to do.

They said they're ordering the CAT scan immediately and would pick us up as soon as they were ready for us. They left the room. I quickly said some Tehillim and said some other prayers in my own words. I interrupted my husband from learning and gave him a quick update. I told him to start getting ready this way as soon as we get picked up there will not be any delay.

My family was getting nervous as they tried calling and messaging us. As I was dealing with Shalva and all the doctors, I wasn't taking any calls. At this point, I quickly messaged them back with a brief update about the blood transfusion and the change of plans. My parents and family were very concerned, and I told them Shalva needed lots of prayers. They all said they'd daven, and they spread her name around for prayers.

My husband closed his Gemara (Talmud) and put his things away while being wrapped up his thoughts. A few minutes later, a resident came to pick us up and led us to the exam room to get a CAT scan. We hurried down the hallways to the elevators as my husband started schmoozing (chatting) with the resident.

I have no clue how the conversation came up, though they started talking about the basketball player who converted to Judaism. My husband started talking about a time that we met him in the Judaica store. When we saw him in the store, my husband approached him and said you look so familiar. The basketball player introduced himself just by his Hebrew name, Yehoshafat Stoudemire, he then went on to say, "I don't know how you'd know me." My husband asked if he's the famous NBA player Amar'e Stoudemire and humbly, he said yes.

My husband was very blown away and inspired by his humility and how he put truth before his fame. They then took a picture together as this was a unique and inspirational moment that my husband cherishes.

We got to the room, and as we put Shalva on the bed, they started wrapping her up. My husband was confused and asked why we were doing a cat scan if we were going on to get an MRI. I looked at him and said, "I told you when I interrupted your learning that the plans were changed, and I updated you." He was so dwelled in his learning that what I said went right over his head, and he couldn't believe it.

He realized now why I've been looking so nervous, and he apologized for going on a tangent. He was in his own bubble. He asked me to repeat everything that was going on, and so I did. They then told us we had to leave the room as they were doing the CAT scan. Shalva was very scared to be left alone, though I reassured her that I was waiting for her outside the door. I told her that as soon as they were done, I was going to come get her. It broke my heart as I left her in tears.

We spent the whole time davening. A few minutes later they opened the door. I quickly ran to Shalva and held her in my arms, and she hugged me so tight. We were led straight to the OR area.

We waited for about two minutes until the surgeon came to us and said they were going to do an emergency surgery. They made us sign another consent in case she needed another blood transfusion. They said they'd get her into the OR any minute. First, the anesthesiologist is going to come for us to sign some consents. Right away, they came, we signed the documents, and minutes later they came to get her. They told us they'd call us as soon as the surgery was over. Being that it was almost the start of the second days of Sukkos, they said if our phones were shut, they'd come to look for us in either the waiting area or our room.

They said we would be transferred to the PICU (Pediatric Intensive Care Unit), and if we were transferred during this time, they would be informed. They then took Shalva straight into the OR.

We both felt frightened, scared, worried, nervous and more. It's hard to pen down the thoughts. We went to the waiting area and didn't waste a moment.

My husband continued to learn his daf (page of the Talmud) as a zchus (merit) for Shalva, as I was saying Tehillim with tears flowing down my cheeks.

My parents called to check up on us and see what's going on. I quickly filled them in, and then spoke to my boys without updating them. I just sent them my love and lots of kisses. I hung up the phone in a hurry as I just wanted to daven. A few minutes later my daughter called me she missed me and wanted to schmooze. I spoke to her for a few minutes. She told me about her day, and she asked what I was doing. I didn't want her to be nervous, so I told her Shalva's going to be okay. She's having a procedure so she can feel better and I'm just waiting and davening. I told her I loved her and missed her and would be thinking about her the rest of Sukkos. With that, we ended the call.

A few minutes later, they called us and told us to transfer to the PICU. We quickly took all our belongings, went with them, dropped our stuff off in the room, and started heading towards the elevators to go back to the waiting area. As we were about to go in the elevator, the surgeons came out. We stood in the hallway, and they spoke with us.

They explained to us that they made a small incision on Shalva's already existing incision line and got out one and a half liters of blood. They couldn't seem to find the source of what was going on. They said that because she lost more blood, they had to give her a blood transfusion. They were scared that the cast on her foot would stop her blood flow, so they had to remove it. They spoke with the orthopedic surgeon, and he was on board. He said he would come to check out her toe at some point during our stay. They also said that

Shalva was in lots of pain and her body was in lots of distress. Being that she had a blood transfusion and had water in her lungs, she needed a breathing tube. They were concerned since it was uncomfortable she might try to pull it out and therefore decided to keep her sedated.

We both felt very frightened, though we were so grateful that we came in when we did, as this was life threatening. It was a really scary time for us. We were asking the surgeons how to prevent this from happening in the future, how did it happen, and a bunch of questions. Being that they didn't know the source of it, they couldn't tell us how to prevent it. They did say that if she falls or bangs into things, there's a possibility that can be a trigger. Though there's no way to know for sure. We just have to pray.

The surgeons hugged me, they really felt our pain. They said they would be there for us, and they really were. We then headed towards the PICU as Shalva was already in there. I walked into the room, and it was the scariest site I've ever seen. Seeing my two-year-old princess hooked onto a breathing tube and monitors was so scary. Minutes before the second day of Yom Tov began my husband said we should get ready to put away our muktzah (items that we are prohibited from using on Shabbos and Yom Tov). I quickly changed, shut off my phone, and put it away.

I then went straight to Shalva's crib and held her hand, kissed her, davened, and talked to her. My heart was in shambles. I was torn into pieces and super emotional. I couldn't fathom how I was seeing her like this. It was so painful seeing her intubated and sedated. I kept crying and wishing to just switch places with her.

In the meantime, my husband went to the Bikur Cholim room. He saw the sign for prayers in the basement of a hotel led by Rabbi Yudi Shmotkin. He came and told me that he was going to daven. He then made his way towards the basement of the hotel for prayers. At this point, my husband needed a shoulder to lean on, and again, the right one, at the right place and at that right moment. Rabbi Yudi Shmotkin was there for a hug, a shoulder to lean on, and a listening ear.

They all prayed and had Shalva in mind. After the prayers were over, they all headed outside to the sukkah for a little festive meal. At that time, my husband got into a great conversation with the rest of the congregants about the existence of G-D, which is a top hit conversation for my husband. Whenever my husband gets caught up in conversations regarding the existence of G-D, proving that no man can ever write the Torah, it gives him a great boost of faith and inspiration that it's all from Hashem.

After that, he came back to us in the hospital feeling uplifted and knowing that everything that's happening right now is all from G-D. It's time to accept, embrace, and be thankful for the situation that we were in. He shared all the conversations with me and gave me a boost of inspiration. We then had a small meal together.

CHAPTER: 16

As the night progressed my husband tried encouraging me to go with him to the chessed apartment we were supposed to sleep by. I was scared to leave Shalva alone, and I told him he should go himself. He left as it was very late, and he was really tired. After he got downstairs, he came back up to try convincing me to come as there was nothing I could have possibly done except daven, but I just couldn't. He felt bad leaving me behind, though I encouraged him to go. I wanted him to have a good night's sleep as we were going through a really hard time. I wished him a good night and told him to walk safely as the streets in that neighborhood were scary, especially late at night.

He reassured me he'd come back to us as soon as he woke up in the morning. He kissed Shalva good night and headed out. I was happy he went to sleep, and I was so scared for Shalva. I was hoping she was okay. I kept asking the nurses, and I was looking at the screen of the monitors. At about 1:30 a.m., I said Shema with Shalva some more Tehillim, kissed her good night, and went to sleep on the couch.

Our room nurse promised me if there were any concerns, she'd wake me up immediately. With that, I fell asleep. I was in a very light sleep, waking up many times to check up on Shalva. In the morning, the nurse told me everything was status quo throughout the night.

At about 8:00 a.m., my husband came to us to see how the night was for both of us. He was glad I got a bit of sleep. He wanted me to walk around a bit. He took me to the bikur cholim room to get a coffee and something to eat.

I had no appetite, though I got a coffee and ran right back up to Shalva as my husband departed and went to Shul.

I couldn't look at Shalva without tears flooding my cheeks. I couldn't sing to her without bursting out crying. I was shattered. I kept davening that Shalva would be healthy, okay, safe, and well. That there should be no complications with anything, that I should have my Shalva back breathing on her own, and that she'd wake up and be healthy.

My husband came home from Shul, and it was time to eat the meal. I told him we would eat in Shalva's room, though I'd go down with him to get the food. That's what we did. I told the nurses we'd be right back, and she said we could take our time.

We got the food and drinks from the bikur cholim room and ran right back up to Shalva's room. We ate the seudah and tried to enjoy it. Seeing Shalva in the state she was in, made it very difficult to enjoy anything. My husband sang some zemiros to try to give me some spirit. He said a D'var Torah and then we bentched.

After we finished eating, one of the surgeons came to check up on Shalva and see how we were doing. She stayed a few minutes and chatted with us. She noticed I was pregnant, as I started to show. She wished me congratulations and told me I had nothing to fear. The baby will be a beautiful, healthy child. I told her I was nervous and hadn't gone to the doctor as we just moved and had to find a doctor in my new neighborhood. I had an appointment scheduled for right after sukkos, but it didn't seem so promising that I'd make it to that appointment.

After the surgeon left our room, I took a walk around the unit. I met two other women who were there with their children. We all shared our stories, as we were all going through our own rough patches. We felt each other's pain. One of the women I met told me something that inspired me for life. Hashem is always with us, holding our hands and guiding us. It's our choice to recognize that or not. When we're in a matzav (situation) like this, Hashem is not only holding our hand, but He is also actually holding us tightly in His arms. He is going through the pain and suffering with us, and we are not left stranded. That is the truth. I always feel Hashem's presence in my life, though when going through these hospital situations, I feel Hashem's presence that much closer. It's because we're in His hands. He's holding us every step of the way. And when I'm not allowed in the OR room with Shalva, I know she's in the best of hands as Hashem is holding her tight.

At this moment, I had a flashback to a previous conversation that we had when we were discussing being on the blacklist. Not only do I not feel like we were on any blacklist, but I also feel privileged and honored to be the mother of such a beautiful and holy soul.

This gave me courage throughout my stay at the hospital and changed me forever. This sticks with me for life. I constantly flashback to the moment that woman told me this. Little did she know the great impact she had on me forever. I came back to the room and shared that with my husband, and it touched his heart.

We spoke a bit, and he went back to his learning as I sat by Shalva's side. I tried talking to her, but I couldn't utter a word out of my mouth as I just broke down in cries. I used the moments of crying to pour my heart out to Hashem and to daven for Shalva's health and recovery.

As the day progressed, I continued davening and completed reciting the entire sefer (book) of Tehillim. There were a few times during the day that Shalva's body jittered. That gave me a sense of relief to know she was okay and alive. Though as soon as she'd jitter, the nurse would quickly up her dose of sedation. They didn't want her to be up yet. They checked the water in her lungs through ultrasounds, and there was still water, so they needed her to continue being intubated and sedated.

Shalva is such a happy, positive, and strong girl. Everyone that knows her sees that she's full of light and life. She lights up all those around her. Seeing her in such a state was unbearable. I kept reminding myself that she is in the best hands right now, she's wrapped in Hashem's arms. That helped me out a lot but seeing her out like the night was still very painful and frightening.

That night was Simchas Torah (it's a very joyous day that we celebrate the conclusion and restart the annual cycle of reading the Torah, dancing and singing with the Torah). My husband went back to the Shul in the basement of the hotel near the hospital. They were trying to accumulate a minyan, waiting around for a very long time.

One of the participating congregants was a man who wanted to say Kaddish (a prayer about faith and giving praise to the Almighty), being that it was one of his parent's yartzeit (the anniversary of the death of a person). It's one of the special times to recite Kaddish, and he didn't want to miss such an opportunity.

As time passed, they were still short of three men, and this individual started to feel anxious and nervous. This might be the very first time he would miss the opportunity of saying Kaddish for his father on his yartzeit. Rabbi Yudi Shmotkin reassured him that Hashem knew he needed a minyan. They started davening without a minyan, skipping the parts that are necessary to say with a minyan. They completed the prayers, and it was time to dance with the Torah. As time went by, he kept on getting more and more anxious and worried as the services were nearing the end.

In the meantime, one of the members went outside for fresh air. As he was standing outside, he noticed a group of religious Jewish men passing by. In this neighborhood it was a very rare occurrence to have a group of Orthodox men walking. At the very moment this man went out for fresh air is when they were passing by. This was no coincidence. The man approached this group of men and told them about their desperate need for a minyan. The men joyfully accepted the invitation and came in to take part of the minyan.

As they came in, the rest of the men were dancing with the Torah and came to a complete pause to witness the miracle that just occurred. With lots of joy, this man jumped up and said the most emotional Kaddish of a lifetime. We all experienced G-D's hands play a role in this beautiful miracle. As Rabbi Yudi Shmotkin really believed there would be a minyan, his Emunah (faith) was so strong that Hashem came through. When we put all our Faith in Hashem, we will never be let down.

The congregants were all happy as they had a beautiful davening ceremony. The man was able to say Kaddish, and they all had an inspiring, uplifting, and joyful Simchas Torah filled with joy, singing and dancing. It was a really uplifting and momentous occasion for everyone at the site. They ended the night with a meal, and my husband made his way back to me.

He came to me all joyful and happy. I knew he went to Shul, and it was Simchas Torah, though the joy on his face was unreal. He then went on to tell me about the most incredible memorable Simchas Torah he's ever had. Being in the hospital for Yom Tov, he was not expecting to have such a beautiful Yom Tov experience. He was glad to say this was one of the most beautiful Simchas Torahs he had experienced in his lifetime.

I was really glad he had such a unique and inspirational experience, as I felt bad that he would miss out on Simchas Torah since we were in the hospital. This was definitely a highlight for him and seeing him so happy made me happy.

It's very important to surround yourself with people who are optimistic, positive and happy. The people you are with have an effect on you without even realizing it. We are influenced by those around us. One small word of acknowledgment, a smile, or some positivity can have such a great impact on others. It's important to greet people with a smile as you may be making their day.

When my husband came into our room all joyful and happy, he had no clue how much that would've had an impact on me. His happiness was contagious, and it lightened up my night. We experienced true Simcha (joy, happiness) on Simchas Torah.

We ate a small meal in our room, and as it was late, my husband was ready to go back to the apartment to go to sleep. He suggested I come with him, and I rejected his offer. I wanted to stay with Shalva. He felt bad leaving me as he knew I wasn't sleeping well in the hospital. I told him I feel the most at home being with my daughter. We said good night and he left the room.

It was about ten minutes later. He came back and told me he couldn't leave me there. He felt it was important for me to get a good night's sleep. He offered to stay with Shalva if that's what I'd feel comfortable with. I told him there was no way I'd take away his sleep. That would be the most selfish feeling, and I personally wanted to be there with her. He told me in order for me to be able to function and take care of Shalva, I have to take care of myself and not neglect my sleep. I saw he was very sincere and decided to go with him to the chessed apartment.

Before leaving, I said Shema (nightly prayer of protection), some Tehillim, and kissed Shalva good night. I told her I'd be back as soon as I woke up. I kissed her again, got so emotional, and started crying. The nurse saw me in tears and promised that someone would come to where we were staying if there were any alarming concerns or emergencies. That was reassuring to me, and I hoped everything would be okay with her.

We went straight to sleep. I woke up throughout the night feeling guilty for leaving Shalva. I was very concerned and worried about her, so I kept having a hard time falling back asleep. Finally, at 7:00a.m. I woke up, jumped out of bed the fastest I've ever had. I woke up my husband and told him we must hurry and get back to Shalva as we hadn't seen her in six and a half hours. Within ten minutes from when I woke up, we were on the way back to the hospital. My husband said we should go get a coffee from the Bikur Cholim room before going to Shalva, but I disagreed. I gave him a choice, he could either go to get a coffee himself while I went straight to Shalva, or he could come with me, so of course he came with me.

I hurried into Shalva's room and made my way directly to her. The nurse was checking in on her as I got there. I asked how she was doing and what was going on with her, how her night was and if there were any updates. She said the night went well, and they're going to be doing another X-ray on her lungs shortly.

My husband then went back to the Bikur Cholim room, made us both a coffee, and brought it up to me. He then left to go to Shul to daven.

I stayed in the room at Shalva's side, davening and saying Tehillim, emotional as can be. I kept asking the nurses and residents that came around "when will I have my Shalva back?" It was so hard as I wanted to hold her in my arms, sing to her, play with her, and nurture her. I felt very helpless and that's an awful feeling for a mother to have.

A few hours passed, and my husband was back from Shul. We had a small meal and took a little walk around the hospital to get a change of scenery.

We came back and stayed with Shalva the rest of the day. The day felt endless. The clock was ticking so slowly that it moved one digit at a time. It felt like forever.

During the day, my husband spoke to Shalva, and she shook her head. That was such a treat for us. We had the reassurance that she was alive and knew what was going on. I felt it was a gift from Hashem to give us some menucha (peace, tranquility). As the nurses saw her moving a little, they quickly hired the dose of sedation, I asked them not to. They said for her safety, they needed to.

As nightfall came and my husband was done his prayers, Simchas Torah came to an end and Yom Tov was over. We went back to the chessed apartment to pack up our things. After we showered, we made our way back to the hospital.

CHAPTER: 17

On the way, I spoke to my parents. They wanted to hear what was going on with Shalva. Before I gave any updates, I told her that I missed my children and asked how they were over Yom Tov. Then I spoke with my boys, and they asked me when I'm coming home. I told them I'd be staying with Shalva, and my husband would come pick them up tomorrow morning.

One of my sons had a very hard time. He was very scared the whole Yom Tov and kept on asking my parents and siblings if something happened to Shalva or if she died. They tried reassuring him that she was alive, and she would be better, though he did not take to it well.

When I spoke with him on the phone, he asked me to send him a picture of Shalva right now, he wanted to see for himself. I was hesitant to send a picture of her in the state she was in as she didn't look lively. It was a very frightening sight for me, how much more so for my young son. I told him she was sleeping now, and as soon as she woke up, I'd try to send over a picture. He wasn't thrilled about that idea, though he accepted it.

That night, we both slept in Shalva's room with her. Well, I didn't really sleep. The night was long, and finally, Thursday morning arrived. I was excited for a new day and was davening that when the sun rises, so should my daughter rise and shine and wake up.

The doctors made their rounds and said if the X-rays were clear today, they would be taking out the tubes. If they see that she can breathe well on her own, they'll wake her up. I felt there was hope and davened that everything should work out perfectly.

My husband was planning on leaving the hospital first thing in the morning. Once he heard this, we discussed it and said he should wait until noon. This way, he can be here when Shalva wakes up.

Shortly after the X-rays were done, we were told they'd take out the breathing tube. I felt so happy! Chasdei Hashem, I'm going to have my princess back. A short while later, they removed the breathing tubes, and Baruch Hashem, she was breathing on her own.

They warned us that when she wakes up, she may be very groggy, cranky, fidgety, tired, and out of it. We should let her sleep as much as she can until all the medicines wear out.

They woke her up, Hodu LaHashem Ki Tov Ki Lolom Chasdo! I was so happy. I felt such relief. As soon as they allowed me to hold her, I picked her up gently and held her in my arms. I was so emotional and felt so blessed! My husband spoke to her a little, took some pictures of her, and told her he'd be back.

He then left to go get my boys, as they were really nervous and homesick. I held her for a while and nursed her to sleep, I kept her in my arms for hours and I didn't want to let go. I missed my gem and felt such Hakaros Hatov (gratitude) towards Hashem that Shalva was up and alive.

In the meantime, my husband picked my boys up from New York and headed back to New Jersey to pick up my daughter.

I spoke to my daughter and told her that my husband and boys were on the way to her. She told me about her Yom Tov and how she was very worried for Shalva. I reassured her that Baruch Hashem Shalva is doing wonderful! And we just need to keep davening for her!

A few hours later, my husband got all the children and took them home. He fed them supper and did bedtime with them. They asked him many questions and he answered them all to the best of his ability with sensitivity.

He told them that after Shalva's surgery, they kept her sleeping until today, they didn't understand what that meant, though the answer satisfied them.

Now that Sukkos was over we had to figure out what to do with the children. Chai Lifeline is an amazing organization that really came full force for us. My sister-in-law contacted them, and they reached out to me. They asked me how they could be of help. I told them the whole situation that I was in. That I'd be staying with Shalva as long as she's admitted. They sent volunteer girls to my house Monday-Thursday to do homework, feed the children, and give the kids attention. They'd send over food to the house for my family and to us in the hospital.

I had wonderful neighbors who also made suppers and offered their help. My boys now had transportation to school, and that was very helpful. Over Chol Hamoed, my sister-in-law made many calls until she finally found a school that would take my four-year-old son. They didn't really have room, though they had a heart and said they'd try it out for a week. My son was so excited to start school. My sister-in-law took him, and he was very excited the whole way there. Though, as soon as she left him, he started to cry.

The teacher was very warm and gave him lots of extra TLC (Tender, love and care). The first day worked out beautifully. My sister-in-law would take him to school, pick him up, and watch him until the boys would get home from school. The volunteer girl would then come to take care of them at home. There was a boy in the class who lived down the block from my sister-in-law. His mother was very kind and generous and offered to take my son and pick him up every day. It was a great arrangement and a massive help.

My husband called me up to discuss Shabbos plans. I told him as much as I would love him to be with me and Shalva, it's more important that he stays home with the children. They had a very hard Yom tov, and they needed some stability.

In the meantime, over Chol Hamoed, another sister-in-law called me up and said she's trying to get my daughter into a school. She spent hours on the phone and in person meetings, though she was still not in school.

My sister-in-law did everything she possibly could to try applying and getting my daughter into school. I started making lots of calls while I was with Shalva in the hospital. All day, I was busy dealing with Shalva and trying to get my older daughter into school.

In the meantime, every day, she'd bounce around from one family to another, in New Jersey and in New York. It was very hard for her not to have me around. Besides that, having no routine or schedule and bouncing around from one house to another was very unsettling.

My husband continued commuting to work and made sure to be home before the volunteer would have to leave. It was a great help, though it was very hard for my children.

My boy's school was incredible. They gave my kids extra TLC and dealt with them with lots of extra sensitivity. They also tried helping us find a school for my daughter. We were in touch pretty much on a daily basis.

Friday, as I was on the phone with my husband, they came into the room to put in a new IV line. I quickly wished him a good Shabbos, sent love to my kids, and hung up the phone. I sat with Shalva as they were poking away, trying to find a good vein. They tried both her arms and then her feet. She was crying in pain as I was crying with her. I felt so bad for the extra torture she's been through.

Over Shabbos, as I was near her, I didn't realize, and I pulled out the IV line in her foot. I started crying hysterically and the roommates heard me. They asked if everything was okay as they saw the whole commotion on Friday with trying to get the IV-line in. As soon as I said the IV-line was out, they understood my pain. They were so nice and caring. They then called in the nurse for me.

The nurse came in and asked why I was in tears. I told them how hard it is for them to find a good vein, and after many tries yesterday, they got it in her foot, and by mistake, I pulled it out. I couldn't bear seeing her go through all this again. She said she'll tell them, though, she'll give her a little break for now and possibly do it while she's asleep.

In the meantime, the nurse came in to check on her vitals. She was already getting annoyed with being checked every few hours, so I asked the nurse if Shalva could switch rolls and do the vitals on the nurse first. They both thought that was a great idea, so that's what they did. We called Shalva Dr. Shalva and let her do the vitals on the nurse. She felt so proud and responsible, and when she was done, she let the nurse do her vitals.

As a mother, it's very important for me to make my children feel safe and comfortable. I don't like to force things, I like to encourage, explain, and sometimes come up with creative ways in which my child feels a part of the decision rather than being forced into it. I obviously won't ask her, hey, do you want surgery or a blood test etc. I'd rather tell her the outcome. That her focus will be on that rather than the fear of the pain.

Later that night, they came in to do it as she was asleep. I knew that this would wake her, so I snuggled her into me, rubbed her arms, and davened that they should get the IV line in a good vein right away on the first try. They said they'd be gentle and only prick her if they really felt they got a good vein. It took a few minutes and Baruch Hashem, they got it in a good vein on the first try.

After Shabbos was over, my husband called me to see how Shabbos was with Shalva and what happened with the IV line. I told him everything, and he felt so bad for everything Shalva's been through. I then asked about the family at home. He said it was a great choice to keep him home as that's what the kids really needed.

The following Monday, the doctors and surgeons were thinking of the next step. They agreed that it would be beneficial to do a three-day round of Sclerotherapy on Shalva. It was scheduled for Wednesday. On Monday and Tuesday, they just kept her monitored and did some imaging and blood work. I got to spend lots of quality time with her.

My daughter kept calling me, nervous about Shalva. She wanted to visit, and her not being in school took a real toll on her emotionally. Chai Lifeline arranged a big sister for her once a week to come and take her out and spend time with her. They arranged another day for her to go rock climbing to keep her stimulated, busy, and happy. It's incredible what they did for her and our whole family. We are forever grateful to them. They were literally a lifesaver. They were there in every way they possibly could be.

Since Shalva was born, I expressed my feelings to many people that I spoke with about how I miss my kids, how I wish I could be there for them, and how they are having a very hard time. They would always respond by saying, Baruch Hashem, the children are all young and resilient. They won't remember any of it.

I don't know if I was vulnerable, naïve, or in denial, though I came to believe that. I was always there for my children and wanted the best for them. At the same time, I felt happy that they were resilient. That must be a coping mechanism for many people to believe that children are resilient. Unfortunately, as time moved on, I saw firsthand that children are not resilient. Children feel what's going on, and every child takes it differently and reacts to situations differently. If you don't nip it in the bud, the trauma they experienced will move on with them for life.

To give an example to help understand how a child's brain molds, try to imagine this. Take a young child's arm and tie it up with a string. Keep it tied until they're fully grown and developed. When the time comes to remove the string, the arm will naturally bend in the way it was their entire childhood years.

The arm learned to adapt to the bent position and that became the norm. It is the same with young children when they go through traumas, without any care. The child will develop thinking patterns in order to cope with what they've been through since it's being swept under the rug. Children are resilient, they are not getting the proper guidance and treatment they need, which can cause lots of emotional distress later on in life.

CHAPTER: 18

Over the weekend, I met some really special Chai Lifeline volunteers in the hospital. They visited Shalva and gave her some toys and prizes. One night, they came to give us donuts. Shalva's face lit up and she was so happy. I'll never forget that smile on her face while she was holding that donut in her hand. She was glowing.

It was a real eye opener, on how a small little thought and gesture of a donut can brighten up someone's day. It's all the small things that people do that make such an impact. When people show their love and concern, it makes a world of difference.

The day passed, and then the next. Tuesday night, after making arrangements for my children at home, my husband came to the hospital. He came to be there with us when Shalva went in for her procedure in the morning. I liked it when he stayed at home with the kids, though procedure days I needed the extra emotional support, so he came to be with us.

As it was nearing midnight, I woke Shalva up to give her a drink and tried feeding her. Being that she had just woken up, she didn't have much of an appetite. I was happy with whatever she ate. After midnight, she wouldn't be able to eat or drink anything until after the surgery. I then put her back to sleep and tried to go to sleep myself. I knew the next day was going to be a big one.

The next morning, my husband woke up bright and early to daven and learn his Daf Yomi (daily page of the Talmud). I told him to make himself a coffee and get something to eat for himself. He should also make sure not to come in with any food or drinks as I don't want the smells to make Shalva thirsty or hearty up her appetite. He offered me, though I declined. I couldn't have the pleasure of a coffee or food while my princess was fasting. I made a decision to fast with her. Except for water, because I was pregnant and wanted to make sure I was fully hydrated. However, I would leave the room to drink. While I tried keeping Shalva asleep, I knew she'd wake up hungry, and she wasn't allowed to eat. I kept the shades closed, the lights off, and made sure it was very quiet in the room. She stayed asleep until the nurses came around to check her vitals.

After the nurse left the room, I tried putting her back to sleep, though she had no intention of closing her eyes. She was up and about. She was hungry and asked for food. I told her that we couldn't eat and had to wait for the doctors. In the meantime, I played with some toys with her, gave her crayons to color, and read her some books. I kept her as occupied as I could.

They came to check her blood. They wanted to make sure her hemoglobin level was okay. Shortly after, they picked us up, and we all headed towards the OR. They had me wear the blue hospital scrubs. Shalva laughed seeing me in them.

We walked her towards the elevators and went down to the unit. We waited with her until they were ready for her. We played with some Legos and read some books. The nurse was very friendly, and Shalva enjoyed playing with her, as long as she was sitting on my lap. She felt secure and content when I held her. Soon, the anesthesiologist came, and I signed the consent forms. They wanted to take Shalva, but she was holding on to me for her dear life. I hugged her as they gave her what they call happy juice to calm her down. It didn't work out as planned and she started looking very oozy and out of it. Yet the moment they tried taking her from me, she started crying and pulled her hands towards me. I couldn't depart from her like this, I asked if I could walk her to the OR, to which they agreed. Outside the OR, they tried taking her again, and she wouldn't go. At that point, I requested that they put her to sleep in my hands. At first, they said I couldn't go into the OR, and that's not an option.

They saw I wasn't comfortable letting go of her looking terrified for her life, so they agreed to do it right outside the OR. I kissed her and said some

Tehillim as they started putting her to sleep. They then quickly took her into the OR and told me they'd call me to meet them when the procedure was over.

During this time, my husband was upstairs in the room learning. I went back to the room and davened. I didn't answer any phone calls as I just wanted to utilize every minute that I could to daven. They called me to tell me the procedure was going smoothly, and I should meet them in twenty minutes. We quickly ran downstairs to the hospital gift shop to buy her a present and headed straight towards the recovery room. Being that they still had some restrictions due to COVID, they only allowed one parent to be with her at a time. I let my husband see her, kiss her, and give her a blessing. Then I told him that since we can't both be here with her in the recovery room, he should go back home to the kids, and I'd stay with Shalva. That's what we did. He left, and I stayed. It took her a few minutes, and she woke up. I held her right away, and she fell back asleep in my arms. We waited some time until they transferred her back to her room.

It was a hard day as she was groggy and blah from anesthesia and in pain. She was on pain meds around the clock. She kept on pointing out the window, asking for my husband. She was hoping he'd be her savior and take her home.

She was very homesick and kept asking when we were going to leave. I kept telling her that we'll go home as soon as she felt better, and we were all davening for her to have a complete and speedy Refuah Shelaima (complete recovery)! She slept a lot that day and didn't eat much.

The next morning, the IR (Interventional Radiologist) came to her bedside and gave her some pain meds. She was going to open her drains and put some medication in there, which can feel very painful with a burning sensation. She waited for the pain meds to kick in, and as I held her on my lap, she did it. Shalva was crying in so much pain and was jumping out of her skin. It tore my heart apart. I was very emotional and reassured her that it was painful, though this was going to help her feel better. When it was completed, they said that Shalva was very irritable, uncomfortable, and in lots of pain. They therefore gave her more pain meds.

It was another long and hard day that was really emotionally draining. My mother came to visit and brought some food, treats, and presents for Shalva. It was a great distraction for her, and it helped her forget about her discomfort and pain.

We have a Mitzvah (One of the 613 commandments in the Torah) of Bikur Cholim (visiting the sick). It's such an important mitzvah, and I really understood it for the first time when I saw how healing it was for Shalva when she had company.

With the hospital rules, you can't have many visitors, though when my mother, husband or Chai Lifeline volunteers came to visit, Shalva's face would light up and glow. When she got phone calls and gifts from family, friends, and Chai Lifeline it really cheered her up and helped her stay busy during the hospital stay.

On Thursday, after the second round of Sclerotherapy, the doctors checked on Shalva. They told us the great news that after the third round tomorrow, she can be discharged. I quickly called my husband to tell him the great news. In the meantime, my sister-in-law in New Jersey invited us all for Shabbos.

Friday morning, they came in to check on Shalva. I asked them what time we were being discharged. They said it depends on when the IR comes to do Sclerotherapy, and we have to wait a bit after that. I reminded them that since it's Friday, I have to be discharged early enough so that I can make it back in time for Shabbos. They told me they'll send over the message.

I packed up all our belongings. This way, as soon as we were discharged, we could leave without a delay. After the kids got home from school and showered, my husband packed them up and dropped them off with their belongings at my sister-in-law's house. He then made his way to the hospital.

In the meantime, the third round of Sclerotherapy was done. They gave her extra pain meds as they saw how painful it was for her the day before. They did all her vitals and started getting us ready for discharge.

My husband called to tell me he was stuck in bumper-to-bumper traffic. I let him know that I was ready to go as soon as he arrived. I got the discharge papers and all the instructions to go home, and then we just waited. In the meantime, my husband called his sister who lives in New York. He told her that depending on the time he arrives at the hospital, there's a possibility we may need to come for Shabbos.

My husband came, and we quickly thanked all the nurses and residents we saw as we headed out with Shalva and all our luggage. We got to the car and saw that it was less than an hour and a half to Shabbos. We would not make it back to New Jersey on time. He quickly called his sister back and told her we had just left the hospital and wouldn't make it to New Jersey in time so we would come to her.

We called my sister-in-law from New Jersey to update her that the plans were changed and that we would go to New York for Shabbos. Now, the plan was to come to New Jersey right after Shabbos, and we would pick up our children. We spoke to my children and told them that we were not going to spend Shabbos together, though hopefully, we will see them after Shabbos. They were disappointed, though there was nothing we were able to do. I told them I really missed them, loved them, and couldn't wait to see them after Shabbos when we would come back to pick them up.

We arrived at my sister in law's house minutes before Shabbos. I took a quick shower and ran to light the Shabbos candles. It was so nice to be out of the hospital. Everyone was happy that she was discharged.

Over Shabbos, she was very playful, though I noticed her coloring was off. My sister and mother came to visit and spend time with Shalva during the day. The day went on, and she looked more and more pale, my husband and I were concerned, though the family members didn't seem to worry.

When Shabbos was over, we thanked my sister-in-law for hosting us, especially with such short notice. We then headed to my brother's house. He had some of my mail since we were in the process of changing our address. He's been collecting our mail from our old house for us.

We got to their house, and they all came outside excited to greet Shalva. I told them I was concerned with how she looked, and they got me their thermometer. We took the temperature of her stomach, and it was 104°f. I knew that was very high, though her forehead was at a regular temperature.

I quickly called the surgeon, and the answering system picked up. I left them a detailed message, and within five minutes, the surgeon called me back. Without having much of a chance to speak, she said we should hurry back to the ER, and again she'd tell them to expect us.

I ran to my brother's house and took a quick shower as my sister-in-law packed us some food to take along. We then headed straight back to the hospital. I then called my sister-in-law and updated her on the situation and told her my husband would be with me in the hospital in the ER until we got admitted. Then he'd go pick up the kids from her house. It was late, and my kids were already asleep, so they found out in the morning.

Once in the ER, they did more imaging blood work and gave her a new PIC line. I told them about all the trauma we experienced with the pricking, and I didn't want Shalva to have to go through it again. They understood me and said they would do an ultrasound on her to find a good vein, This way they wouldn't need to prick her more than once. I was so happy I opened my mouth and told them how I felt. I was grateful that they acknowledged my emotions by doing the ultrasound. Baruch Hashem, it worked beautifully, and they were able to find a good vein and prick her just once.

We were finally admitted early Sunday morning. The surgeon didn't normally work on Sundays, though she came in special to check up on Shalva. She then told me that when she heard that the temperature was 104°f, she didn't realize that it was on her stomach, she thought it was a fever. She explained that it's not accurate to take a temperature of the stomach, though she appreciated that we thought out of the box.

She said they're going to monitor her, and after they get all the imaging and blood work, they will keep me posted on what is going to happen. Then, my husband left to go pick up our children to be with them.

Besides our regular team of Surgeons, they had a Hematologist come and speak to me. They said they were going to do a more extensive blood test to see if there's anything else going on and to see if there's anything she can do on her end to care for Shalva.

Later that day, they sent Shalva for X-rays. When I came back up, the nurse told me the doctors would come to meet me soon. I went for walks around the unit with Shalva to give her a change of scenery. She was so playful and happy to be able to walk around a little.

As we were walking, we saw a group of doctors nearing our room. I told Shalva we had some doctor friends who wanted to talk to us. We all got to her room at the same time. They spoke to us and asked me some questions and what my concerns were. Then they said they couldn't seem to get to the bottom of this, though they're going to start her on antibiotics to prevent any cellulitis or blood infections. They also said that tomorrow, when the surgeons are in, we will see if they want to do any intervention and what they think. In the meantime, she'll be kept monitored.

Being that I didn't really have any updates, I just davened. It was already the night, so we went to sleep. We were overly exhausted.

CHAPTER: 19

The next morning the IR, surgeons, and doctors came to check on Shalva. They all said for now, they just wanted to keep her monitored for a few more hours, and if she didn't regress, she could be sent home. As much as I missed my children, the comfort of my own home, my bed, my shower, and daily routines, I was nervous to go home.

A few hours passed, and they came to tell me that we would be discharged. Shalva still didn't look well. Being that her case is so unique, when something goes wrong, we end up back in the hospital. I did not feel confident with this decision, though they said if there were any concerns, I should call or email them immediately. They wanted me to come back on Friday for a follow up appointment.

I called my husband to update him, and that we needed to be picked up. He said it would take a while as he can't keep on asking his family for favors. He said he would pick up the kids from school, get something to eat, and make his way to us. It will be a couple of hours.

We waited very patiently. As much as I couldn't wait to see and be with my family, I was feeling really nervous. However, there was nothing I could do about this except to daven, so that's what I did. Hours passed, and my husband updated me with his ETA when he was about twenty minutes away. I made my way down to the lobby with Shalva and our belongings.

The kids were so happy to see us, and especially to see Shalva. It was a moment they needed. They needed to see firsthand that she was okay, safe, healthy, and well. They were talking and singing to her the whole way home.

We got home, and it was already late. We fed the children supper, bathed them, and put them to bed. I was nervous about putting Shalva to sleep in her bed, so I kept her in my room for the night. The next day, my neighbor called and told me she made us dinner. Another neighbor came at lunchtime with a yummy delicious cinnamon bun and frozen coffee colada and told me her family is there for us.

My husband was back with his work schedule, commuting back and forth. My boys were all in school, and my daughter was home with me as she still hadn't gotten into any school. My daughter enjoyed the attention and quality time spent with me and Shalva. She expressed all her emotions and feelings about how she's been this whole time. It was not easy and was so heart breaking.

I told her I was doing everything I possibly could in my power to get her into a school. I was davening, and we just had to be patient until a school had mercy on us. In the meantime, I did some schoolwork with her so she shouldn't fall behind. I got some worksheets and books and had her write her own little diary just to keep her up to par.

It was very hard adjusting back to a regular routine without help and with being extra cautious with Shalva. The week felt everlasting. Tuesday, she didn't look well, though it wasn't such a regression. Wednesday and Thursday, she looked worse. I sent pictures to the surgeon, and they said since we were coming in on Friday, just wait until then, and we will discuss it in person. Thursday came, and she looked even worse, and I just couldn't wait for the next morning to arrive.

Finally, Friday came. The boys went to school, and my daughter went to a family member. We made arrangements for the children when they came home from school to go to my sister-in-law. We then made our way towards New York to the hospital. I was looking forward to this appointment as I was nervous having Shalva home. I was hoping we'd have some more clarity.

We got to the hospital, waited for a short while, and met with the surgeon and IR. We told them all our concerns from the week, they then examined Shalva and spoke with us. They said Shalva does not look well. Although, being that Shalva has been through so much recently, they felt the best thing is for her to give her body some time to rejuvenate. Give it a few months, and her body will be a bit stronger. Then they'll plan for another debulking surgery.

I was not comfortable with this as I felt scared being home with her and not knowing what to do if something were to Chas V'shalom (G-D forbid) happen. I told the doctors, which they understood, though they said if she were to be here, all they would do is keep her monitored as her body went through so much and is too weak. They said I can always call and email them, if need be, and they'll have their office staff call me to schedule a surgery. I didn't feel at ease, though we thanked them as we headed out.

We got to the car and headed back to pick up our children. On the way, we were discussing the appointment. My husband said, they are the professionals, they are the doctors and even though our princess's case is unique, they are a lot more educated than us. If this is the guidance they're giving us, then that's what's meant to be. They are just messengers from Hashem. I heard his point of view, though my gut feeling was telling me otherwise. I was feeling very uneasy. We decided that in any case, it's Friday and we have to pick up our kids and get ready for Shabbos. We will see what happens.

Shortly after, we were all home, settling back in, bathing the kids, cleaning, and preparing the house for Shabbos.

My neighbors were incredible. They arranged for Shabbos food to be sent over. We got really yummy homemade gourmet food, desserts, and platters from some of whom I've never met. As they dropped off the food, they came with warm smiles, and supportive and open hearts. It was so special to see how caring others were.

Friday night, after everyone was in bed I spoke to my husband and shared my concerns. He reminded me that we did all our hishtadlus (efforts) we possibly could. We were davening, took Shalva to her surgeons, and for now, let's just try to enjoy Shabbos.

I carried Shalva into my room and went to bed. I remember lying down and just talking to Hashem. Crying in tears, begging Hashem to guide us and that Shalva should have a complete and speedy Refuah Shelaima. I literally poured out my heart until I shattered into tears. I cried out to Hashem, saying Hashem, you put us through this challenge. I have faith and know you'll guide us through this. I asked Hashem to give me all the energy and courage I needed as I fell into deeper tears. I said some Tehillim until I settled down to say Shema and went to sleep.

All Shabbos, I was trying to reassure myself that everything was okay, and with the help of Hashem, Shalva would be alright. My husband tried comforting me, and when he saw that wasn't helping, he tried distracting me with other conversations. I conversed with him, but Shalva was on my mind the entire time.

Throughout the day, Shalva was complaining about her stomach, and when I looked at it, it looked inflamed and felt hard and warm. I was really not at ease.

When Shabbos was over, I again decided to email one of the surgeons. She said the warmth and hardness are a local inflammatory reaction from the Sclerotherapy, and as long as she doesn't have a fever, this is expected. She didn't seem concerned, which made my husband feel more confident that she was going to be okay. Yet my gut feeling was not accepting this.

I went to bed begging Hashem to guide me and to take care of my princess. I was not taking to this well, seeing my daughter in so much discomfort and pain. I felt so helpless that there was nothing I could do for her. It was an awful feeling.

I had a very restless night of sleep and woke up constantly throughout the night. I kept checking up on Shalva and had a hard time falling back asleep. I just wanted the night to pass and the sun to rise, hoping a new day would come with new blessings!

The sun rose, and I woke up shortly after. While it was still early in the morning, I spoke to my husband and told him I wanted to call someone to get a second opinion. At first, he was hesitant as we were already comfortable with the doctors and surgeons. They gave us such love and cared for us so well. The commute was about one and a half hours away from our house. However, when he saw how worried I was, he agreed that I call.

I called someone from an organization that I spoke with in the past. I updated him with everything that's been going on with Shalva and asked him for guidance. He strongly recommended we go to Boston Children's Hospital, and he'll be there for us every step of the way until we are there. I told him I'd discuss it with my husband and get back to him shortly.

I spoke to my husband, and he was not on board. He was very concerned that it would break the family apart. It was hard enough to commute one and a half hours to the hospital we have been going to. This new hospital, without traffic, was close to being a five-hour commute. He said it wouldn't be fair to the children for me to be so far away from them. He then said he'd call a close family member who's a pediatrician and ask him for advice.

I honestly didn't care what advice anyone would say. I just wanted my daughter to be healthy and well. I wanted her to get better, and I was afraid to just wait around. In the meantime, I called my parents. They were very supportive and on board. They even offered to drive me and Shalva to Boston. Another sister-in-law I spoke with was also on board and was telling me to go. I said I was ready as soon as my husband was on board.

My husband spoke with the close pediatrician family member. He said if the surgeons saw her and were comfortable with her being home, then he agrees there's no reason to schlep all the way to Boston. My husband sounded excited telling me this, though the look on my face spoke more than a million words. He knew that I wasn't giving up so easily.

My husband said I should call the man who suggested we switch hospitals up. I should ask him how he feels about it and about the conversation he just had with our close family member, so I did. He suggested we have a phone conference with me, my husband, my parents, the close pediatrician family member, and himself. I thought that it was a great idea to give everyone a chance to voice themselves. We set up a time and he gave me the conference number.

I informed everyone about the meeting and gave them the time and phone number. I confirmed that it was good for everyone as it was important, and everyone prioritized that the time worked for them.

Being that it was Sunday, my kids looked forward to spending the day with the family. We tried to do an outing or something fun with them every Sunday since they were little. Sunday in our home was called Sunday Funday. While I was awaiting the phone conference, my sister called to say that she was in town and wanted to stop over to see us. So, without telling her anything that was going on, she said she'd come right over with pizza for everyone.

She came right on over and saw me and knew something was up. She asked if I was okay, and I broke down in tears. She offered to drive me to New York to my parents for them to take me, and she offered to be there for me. I appreciated her offer but told her I couldn't go without my husband being fully on board. I said I'd wait until after the phone meeting and have a better idea of what was going to be.

My husband then took the children to Urban Air, which is a trampoline park. I opted to stay home with Shalva, and my sister stayed over for a while. Her heart was broken seeing me like this. She just wanted the best for everyone.

Finally, the time for the phone conference arrived. I called in immediately and we waited until everyone called in. I sent a reminder text, and within five minutes, everyone was on the call. Being that my husband was at Urban Air, he went to the locker area to come on this call.

The phone meeting began with him speaking and asking the close pediatrician family member why he felt we didn't need to go to Boston. He said that based on the fact that surgeons weren't concerned, he didn't feel the need for us to travel so far. I then added in some of my input and feelings. I'm not sure if he knew that Shalva's hemoglobin numbers were really low. She needed a blood transfusion in the hospital during our stay, and she looked very pale. I was scared as her numbers were low again.

After hearing that, he sounded frightened. The conference continued, and someone recommended we first do blood work to see her hemoglobin numbers. I told them I had already done it today and was just waiting for the results. Everyone came to an agreement with that, and then when the results are back, we will head to the hospital. I thanked him and all the participants in the conference call and hung up the phone.

I then tried getting a hold of the blood work. I told them I needed it ASAP. Within the hour, they sent it to the PA, who sent the results straight to me. Her hemoglobin numbers were 6.9, which was low, and it was recommended that we should be seen.

I quickly called my husband and updated him with the results. I told him to come home right away with our kids, and I'll make arrangements for them. My husband said the kids are having the time of their lives, and it's so healthy for them. He was going to give them a few more minutes while I packed up for everyone and made arrangements.

I called my sister-in-law and updated her that my husband was on board, and I told her about the meeting and the plans. I asked her if she could have my children for the night and take them to the bus in the morning. She told me not to worry and I should just go.

I packed up pajamas and clothing for the next day for the kids. For me and Shalva, I packed a few days' worth of clothing. While I was packing, I heard the doorknob twisting and turning as my children and husband came back home. I asked them about Urban Air, and they told me about all the fun they had. I was so happy for them. I then told them that Shalva was still not feeling well and that we were going to be going to a different hospital far away with her.

They started asking many questions and were nervous. I reassured them that with Hashem's help, the new hospital would be a great Shaliach (messenger) from Hashem to make Shalva better. They saw that Shalva was in pain and felt so bad for her. Though they were sad we were going to the hospital since they knew they couldn't come, and they'd miss us. I told them they'd be in good hands for the night. They will be by the cousins, and hopefully, tomorrow night, Daddy will be home and stay with everyone at home.

I then bathed the children and got them ready to go. As the kids were doing their last-minute preparations to leave, my sister and brother-in-law came over as they were in town. My brother-in-law knew lots of resources and offered to help, and my sister offered to be there for the kids and me in any way possible. As soon as everyone was ready, they came out and said hi. I then hugged my sister and had to rush out.

We packed up the car, seat belted all the children inside and headed to my sister-in-law to drop them off. My kids were very sad. I told them how much I love them and will miss them and won't stop thinking of them. I told them I'd speak with them at least every morning before they went to school, when they get home from school, and before they go to bed. I kissed them all as they left the car.

My husband started driving, and a family member called him. She was super anxious in a massive panic, saying, "I heard Shalva's numbers are low. Don't go all the way to Boston and get a blood transfusion locally first." Being that she was in such a panic of fear, it caused my husband to really get nervous and worried. I told her to calm down. We are being guided and doing as we're told.

When we hung up the phone, my husband started getting nervous. I reminded him that the only reason we were even going to the hospital now was because I wanted the best for my daughter. I wanted her to be healthy and well and okay. I gave a little flashback to him of how he and some family members thought this wasn't necessary. I then told him I'd call a PA that knew Shalva well. I'd also call my brother-in-law, who's involved with Hatzalah (Jewish Volunteer medical service) and the amazing man that helped us get to Boston and see what they'd suggest.

The next little while I spent making phone calls. I was basically told to sit in the back next to her and keep a close eye on her. Check her temperature, keep her hydrated, and if at any point she seemed to look worse then go to the closest emergency room or call Hatzalah or 911.

They suggested continuing the journey as we want to get to Boston ASAP. The reason they were okay with us traveling is because when we left the hospital a couple of days prior, her hemoglobin numbers were only a tad higher.

A few of his family members kept on calling my husband in a panic, which caused my husband distress. I told him to pick up and tell them that everything would be okay. If he sounded calm, hopefully, that would calm them down. So, he answered and updated them that we got medical guidance, and everything will work out. Everyone should calm down and daven. They seemed very intense, and my husband then ended the phone conversation with them.

We then continued on our long journey. I sat next to Shalva and kept checking her temperature, her breathing, and her skin coloring. I said some prayers. In the meantime, I got in touch with Chai Lifeline and updated them on what was going on. They arranged for volunteers to continue coming every night while I was in Boston with Shalva, and they'd send over food.

I spoke to a Rabbi who was helping me try to get my daughter into school. He gave me some phone numbers of organizations that place people to sleep and give food during the hospital stay. He gave me lots of resources and told me he'd be davening for Shalva, and he's continuing to work really hard to get my daughter into school.

I felt nervous going to a new hospital, meeting all new doctors, and starting all fresh. At the same time, I was hoping that I'd have more answers and clarity and that they would be the perfect shaliach to help Shalva get better.

My husband had mixed emotions. He was worried from when he spoke with his siblings. He was nervous that we were going to be so far apart, how it was going to split up the family, and the impact it could have on our relationship. I kept telling him if Shalva is going to do well and get better, there will be no regrets. I said, "this is where Hashem is guiding us now, so as nerve wracking as it is, let's daven and work on strengthening our faith that this will be a great decision that we made."

Shalva fell asleep and stayed asleep the whole car ride. We continued talking and sharing our feelings, thoughts, worries, and concerns. After a while, we listened to some music to keep us in a more upbeat spirit.

CHAPTER: 20

We arrived at the hospital at around 1 a.m. We checked in and started the whole process of filling out papers and answering questions. They checked her vitals, and after that they had us wait in the waiting area until we'd be led into the ER.

During the wait, Shalva was looking around, confused about where she was. We told her we had come to a different hospital, and we would be making new friends there with different doctors and nurses.

As we were waiting, she saw many others waiting as well. She saw all the different people there, and I explained that everyone that we see is here for a different reason. Some may have booboos, some may not feel well, some are sick, and we should daven for everyone. She felt so bad for them.

I fed her some snacks that we took along from the house, and she looked out the window a bit, at all the cars that were coming and going from the hospital.

After about an hour, we were called into the ER, and they led us to our unit. The nurses came to do the vitals and asked why we were there. We told them everything that Shalva's been through the past three weeks and my concerns. I then asked them to check her blood work as her hemoglobin numbers were low. A nurse right away put in an order for that.

The doctors came around one by one, and we kept repeating Shalva's whole situation to them. Shortly after they came in to do blood work, I told them that her veins are very hard to find and that she always ends up getting tons of pricks until they find a good vein. I said she's been through so much, and it's so heartbreaking for me to see her experience extra pain and discomfort.

They said they'd check her veins and if they can't find a good vein right away, they will not prick. They will bring an ultrasound to help guide them. I was very comforted by that. They checked, didn't see a good vein, and they kept to their word. They said they'd be back shortly with an ultrasound machine.

A few minutes later, they were back, all prepared with the ultrasound machine. Shalva was very scared, so I snuggled her into me and told her that I'd be holding her. My husband would hold her hand and she could squeeze as tight as she needed. The nurse came in with a device, put on Baby Shark, and let Shalva start watching before they even began. They wanted to keep her distracted and calm.

The nurses were super friendly and sweet. Shalva felt safe and had the support from all of us. They then did the ultrasound and found a good vein. She felt the pinch and got scared. We reassured her that it was good they got it, and by the time the song was over, she'd be done with the blood test. Baruch Hashem, it worked out well.

When they all left the room, we closed the lights to try putting Shalva back to sleep and for us to get some rest. Shalva fell asleep right away, and my husband closed his eyes for a bit while I was trying to show the records from the previous hospital to them from my patient's portal. I sent them a request to send this hospital her entire file.

The night was long, and I was exhausted. I tried to rest a bit, though every time I'd fall asleep, they'd come in for vitals, or results, or have us go down to get an ultrasound. There was a lot going on the entire night. They said we would be admitted.

The night was long, and we were all exhausted. At about 8:30 a.m., we were finally admitted into a room. As we were settling into the room, a nurse came to introduce herself. We opened up the couch as a bed so we could finally get some sleep. We were all so exhausted from the travel and from being up all night in the ER.

As I almost fell asleep, we got a phone call from the extraordinary man who arranged for us to go to Boston. My husband thanked him for everything and updated him. We then put our phones on silent mode, I put Shalva to sleep, and we all took a nap.

It wasn't long until the nurses came around for vitals. The residents made their rounds, introduced themselves and asked us many questions. I was so exhausted I couldn't think straight. At one point, I just wished I had recorded myself and would be able to replay the recording to each new resident, doctor, surgeon, and nurse that would come in. Though that wouldn't really be realistic, we just desperately needed sleep.

Throughout the day, meeting with all the residents and doctors, they said that they were part of the weekend staff and that tomorrow there will be new shifts of doctors that will join our case. They said that they would relay all the information over to them. In the meantime, they will do some imaging and give Shalva a pic line. This way, they would get blood straight from the pic line, and if she needed any meds, they would give it to her through the IV line as well.

They again got the ultrasound machine in the room to insert a pic line in Shalva's arm, and they did it. She was scared, though she remembered it from in the middle of the night. We again gave her all the support the nurses were all very soothing and patient with Shalva as they inserted the pic line.

My husband decided he'd stay with us until we came up with a game plan. That night, someone from the Boston Jewish community spoke with my husband and said his wife made supper for us. he said he'd be going to Shul, so my husband said he would meet him there.

A couple of minutes later, my husband went to a Shul nearby to daven Mincha and Maariv (afternoon and evening prayer services) and met that man whom he became friendly with. While he was out, the nurse came to me with an update that Shalva could not eat past midnight as she was going to go through an MRI In the morning. I then said Shema with Shalva and put her to sleep.

They came in with consent forms and told me she'd be put under anesthesia. I was hesitant as it's not healthy, especially at such a young age, and I didn't want her to be affected cognitively. They heard me out and explained they needed her to be asleep. I asked if they could give her Benadryl or melatonin. They thought that was a cute suggestion, though they needed her in a deep sleep so that she wouldn't move. I understood, and I tried my best, though if this is what has to happen, I would sign, and so I did.

When my husband came back, Shalva was already asleep, and I gave him the update. We ate supper. It was really refreshing, tasty, and nutritious. My husband thanked the man for the delicious and thoughtful meal, and then he went straight to sleep.

I was very tired, though I tried to keep myself up until 11:00 p.m. so I could wake Shalva up to feed her and give her drinks. I dozed off into a light sleep in between and set my alarm just in case. Finally, at 11:00, I woke her up, fed her a little, gave her a drink, and put her back to sleep, and then I went straight to sleep.

In the morning, we met the new nurse and, throughout the day, met different residents from different teams of doctors and surgeons. They all spoke with us, and they said they would come up with a plan after they get the results from the MRI and speak it over with us.

The morning was rough as Shalva was hungry, though shortly after, we took her down for an MRI. While we were waiting for her turn, I explained to her that she was going to be put to sleep, and while she was sleeping, the doctors were going to get lots of pictures of the booboo. When she was in the MRI, I used my time to daven.

When the MRI was done, we were led to the recovery room to meet her and be by her side as soon as she awoke. She woke up pretty quickly, and they transferred us back in to her room.

She was very drowsy and out of it for a while, and it took her some time to get back to herself. I snuggled with her as she was jumping out of her skin. I tried to soothe her and have her sleep off the anesthesia.

She then fell into a deep sleep for a few hours. When she woke up, she was still tired, though she was pretty much back to herself. I slowly fed her light and soft foods to make sure she could stomach it, and she did. She had a nice hearty appetite and ate a full meal. I was so happy she was back to herself.

I then read her some books and played with some toys with her. I forgot to mention there is an incredible woman in Boston. I'm not sure if it's an organization or if it's her that runs it, though I spoke with her as soon as we were admitted. She sent over two days' worth of food at a time and some activities and toys to entertain Shalva.

Being in the hospital with a loved one, a child so close and dear to my heart, was so heartbreaking and emotional. It was very difficult seeing her going through everything. I lived through the experience with her and was there with her every step of the way. It was not easy, though the organization really came through. The one in Boston provided us with kosher meals, as there was no Bikur Cholim room in the hospital. They called me to provide support over the phone and see how they can be helpful. Chai Lifeline took care of my children at home by providing volunteers to be there with them, sending over suppers, and calling me to give me support. It was really special and beautiful to see the love and care of the Jewish community. It touched my heart!

Later on in the day, a resident came in with updates that the doctors read the MRI report. The teams discussed that they would like to proceed with Sclerotherapy. I told them the previous hospital thought debulking would be the next option in a couple of months. She said for now, they don't want to be so invasive and prefer to start with Sclerotherapy. If they have my consent, they will start the three-day round tomorrow, Wednesday, and we agreed.

After she left, my husband and I discussed it. I told him that he should stay with me until they did Sclerotherapy the next day, and he did. That night, again, I woke Shalva up at 11 p.m. to eat and drink and put her back to sleep.

Early the next morning, they did her blood work and vitals. They had me sign a consent that if she were to lose too much blood during the procedure, I'm okay with a blood transfusion. As scary as it is, it's scarier not to get it when her life was possibly dependent on it. I signed it without any hesitation as I knew her life was so precious.

My husband went to Shul to daven and then spent many hours learning his daf (page of the Talmud) in the hospital. We took her down to the waiting area by the OR. I explained to her that they were going to put her to sleep and try to make the booboo feel better and take some of the booboo away. I reassured her that she'd be sleeping, I'd be davening, and my husband would be learning in her zchus (merit).

The nurse gave her some toys, so I sat on the floor and played with her. When she didn't want to play anymore, I sat on a chair and held her on my lap. I read her books and spoke to her. I gave her lots of love and attention.

When they were ready, they came in to give her some happy juice to help her stay relaxed and calm when they'd take her from my arms. They tried, but with no success. She looked so oozy and out of it. As soon as they took her from me, she started crying hysterically. I took her back in my arms and asked if there was any way they could put her to sleep on me. They said since I was pregnant, I definitely could not enter the OR room. Though I could walk them

131

until the doorway, and they'd put her to sleep by the doorway in my arms and then quickly transfer her to the OR. I was very appreciative and happy that they were so accommodating. I did that and waited in Shalva's room. They said they'd call me as soon as the procedure was over.

I ran back to the room and told my husband I'd like him to be here with me until Shalva woke up and was transferred back to this room. Then it was very important that he would go home to be with our children.

I spent the time davening until my phone rang. They informed me the procedure was going well and I should meet the doctor in the waiting area in fifteen minutes. We quickly ran to the elevators and made our way downstairs.

We sat down in the waiting area, and a few minutes later, the IR came and spoke with us. He told us it went smoothly and well with no complications. He explained to us in detail what he did in the OR and what to expect during recovery. He answered lots of our questions and was very sensitive and informative. He then led us to the recovery room to be with Shalva.

When we got to the recovery room, the nurse said only one parent could be there at a time. I told my husband he should go give Shalva a hug and kiss and talk to her first, since we both can't wait together. Then he should gather his things from Shalva's room and all our laundry, take it straight to the car, and head back home to be there for our children. With that, I thanked him for everything, and he left.

I sat by Shalva's side for about half an hour until she woke up. Then I held her in my arms a little bit, until she started jumping around. I didn't want the monitors to tangle so I put her down gently and sang to her.

About another twenty minutes later, she woke up, and they called a nurse to transport us back to her room. We got to her room, and I sang her songs until she fell asleep. I kept the lights off and my phone on silent to keep her in a peaceful, calm sleep. I wanted her to wake up when her body was ready to wake rather than be woken up.

CHAPTER: 21

Backtrack a little, I kept to my word fully with my children. I spoke to each one of my children every morning, after school, before they went to bed, and a few times in between. All my kids took it in different ways, it was very hard and challenging. I bought them many gifts from Amazon and had them delivered to my house. I said it was from me and Shalva and that brought them some excitement. Chai Lifeline also sent over gifts which brought such joy to my children.

They kept asking for updates, what was going on with Shalva, if she was okay, and how's her booboo. They asked lots of questions about the procedure and when we would be coming home. So, Wednesday morning, before all the children went to school, I told them all that I had great news for them. Daddy was coming home today. They were very excited, though they really wanted me and Shalva back home as well. I told them I wanted to come home. I missed them all so much more than they can begin to imagine. Now I have to stay in the hospital until Shalva is healthy enough to be back home.

Being that my daughter was not in school, it was extremely difficult for her. Every day she was somewhere else. My heart was torn, and every single day in the hospital, I spent hours making calls trying to get her into a school. I also shed many tears asking Hashem for guidance to get my daughter into school.

Shalva woke up, and after a little while, asked for Daddy. I said he had to go home to take care of the other children. She started crying that she wanted Daddy to take us home. I told her that we had to stay in the hospital until her booboo felt a little better, and I promised I was going to stay with her the entire time.

With feeling so emotional, experiencing everything with Shalva, my daughter not in school, and my children having a hard time, I was very heartbroken and emotionally overwhelmed. To top it all off, there was some major drama going on. Instead of being emotionally loved and supported, I had to deal with lots of drama, which caused lots of stress and that was not easy.

Baruch Hashem, I did have great support from family and friends. I was very thankful and grateful to Hashem for that. In times like these, I got to see some true colors of people and all the trauma and distress it caused me. I appreciated that it was a blessing from Hashem! I got the clarity, the true colors shined, and I saw who each person really was. The truth came out.

My heart was in shambles, and I was torn. I remember one night after I put Shalva to sleep, I curled under my pillow and blanket, crying to Hashem, saying I felt like I was being stormed by tornadoes, hurricanes, thunderstorms, gunshots, and bombs all at once. I couldn't make sense as to why I had all this pain and suffering coming from all different directions at the same time. I was torn and felt all alone.

I calmed myself down, saying Hashem has a Master plan and I don't understand it. Though there's nothing that happens in life that shouldn't happen. It was destined by Hashem, and there was nothing in my power or control that was possible for me to do to not be in this situation with everything happening all at once. G-D is Perfect and if I'm meant to suffer, I accept it as a kappara (atonement).

This calmed me down so that I was able to sleep. Though I had moments where my Emunah (faith) wasn't as strong, and I felt crushed and crumbled to pieces. No matter how I felt, I was with Shalva and put her first. I didn't let my feelings come in the way of my love and care for Shalva. I knew part of my mission was to be here wholeheartedly and give my all to Shalva, so I did.

Until this very day, I find it so mind boggling that when those people saw me suffering and in the hospital with a child and knew everything that was going on and what we were experiencing, they were able to act in such a way. I felt such rejection that not only were they not there for me in the slightest possible way, but they also treated me as if they didn't know anything I was experiencing and shoving me under the rug with all the drama. It was a real pain, a sharp stab right in the center of my heart. It really hurt. I forgive them all. The only way I can possibly make sense of this situation is that being that they'd never been in my shoes, Baruch Hashem, they didn't realize to be sensitive and caring.

The drama was so bad that even if it would've happened at a calmer time in my life, it would still have been very traumatic and hard to stomach and deal with. I bless them all that they should never be put in such a situation and never be able to understand me firsthand. Though I daven that they never do such a thing to anyone else, especially when they're going through such hardships. I moved on, and I forgave, though anytime this memory comes up, my body cringes.

There's a time and place for everything, though I definitely didn't feel that this was it. At the end of the day, I know Hashem needed me to go through all of this at once, and they were sent to be the messengers to cause me the extra pain. At the moment, it was very difficult, though in the long run, I learned many valuable lessons in life. It definitely helped me grow and strengthen myself. During this time period, I was weaker, but as time progressed, I learned that no one can put me down or take me down unless I put myself in their arms. I learned to stand up for myself and my values and wouldn't let anyone break me apart.

My kids have one mother, and that's irreplaceable. I have a mission to be the best mother I can possibly be in order for my children to blossom and grow into the most beautiful, amazing, individual, and unique children each one of them are.

Wednesday night was the same protocol as the night before. No eating past midnight. I woke Shalva up to feed her and put her back asleep until the morning.

Thursday morning, we woke up bright and early and they did vitals on Shalva. I told them that Shalva keeps complaining that the pic line is too tight and that it's hurting her. They got the team in the room to check it out, and her whole arm blew up and was red and swollen. They quickly applied ice to her arm as they wanted to make sure her blood flow continued. They were glad that I spoke up on Shalva's behalf, which is what I always did. I'm Shalva's biggest advocate.

As some nurses were dealing with the swollen arm, others went to get an ultrasound to put in a new pic line on the other arm or foot, depending on where they'd find a good vein. She was crying in pain, as I was crying along with her, rubbing her face and davening for her. I was heartbroken.

After a few minutes, they were done, and they left us with an ice pack and said they'd keep coming to check on that hand. In the meantime, there was an emergency, and the IR was working on another patient, so we had to wait.

Shalva was so hungry and kept on asking for something to eat or drink. I fasted along with her and told her we couldn't eat until the doctor saw her and took care of her booboo after the procedure. She kept asking me to call the doctor as she just wanted something to eat.

I played with her and read to her. I tried napping with her, and she slept for about an hour. Though as soon as she woke up, she wanted food. I felt so bad saying no. I told her we would go for a walk and see if we saw any doctors, so we did. We walked in circles around our unit. She was so friendly with the nurses in the hallway. When we saw her nurse, I asked for updates. She kept saying that, hopefully, as soon as there was an update, she'd inform me immediately.

We kept walking. some nurses gave Shalva stickers, others gave her a balloon, and we looked out the window at the scenery. Finally, it was about 1:30 p.m., and the nurse said we should start getting ready because Shalva was scheduled for 2:00. They'd be coming in any minute to get her.

We hurried back to her room and waited on her bed. I gave her a little prep talk as to what we were about to do. I told her the nurses were going to come, they may check her vitals, and then they're going to lead us to the elevators to the waiting area.

A few minutes passed, and we were in the waiting area with the same nurse as the day before. Shalva right away sat down on the floor to start playing with toys and I accompanied her and played with her. Again, the anesthesiologists came in, spoke to me, I signed the consent forms, and shortly after they were ready for her.

Being that the happy juice didn't help the day before, I requested them not to give it to her. They wanted to try giving it to her a little earlier so that it had more time to kick in. I figured they knew better, and we should try. And so, they did.

Shortly after, they tried taking Shalva out of my arms, and she held on to me so tightly, she squeezed her hands around my neck. She just wanted me. At that point, they said I should walk them outside the OR room, and they'd put her to sleep in my arms like they did yesterday. That was such a relief. I was so happy as I didn't want Shalva to have to experience any unnecessary or extra distress.

I went to the waiting area and said some Tehillim until I got the call that the procedure went well. I met with the doctor and then was led to the recovery room. They gave her a smaller dose of anesthesia, so she woke up sooner. We were then transferred back to her room.

The drama didn't stop between calls and messages, it was insane. I tried to stay strong, though it was not easy. I felt as if I was walking through a dark forest in thunderstorms with animals surrounding me. Feeling trapped and lost, not knowing which way to turn or go to return to safety. These feelings were intense and real, though it was nothing anyone was able to understand. I tried getting guidance from our Rabbi, though with all the circumstances I was in, it was really hard for me to get all my feelings out.

In the meantime, my husband was overwhelmed being home, having to take care of all the children. From early in the morning waking, dressing, and feeding them, to taking them to the bus stop, driving my four-year-old to school, picking him up from school, and keeping my daughter entertained. He wasn't able to go to work as he had to take responsibility over the children and house. It was not easy for him.

I was always a stay-at-home mom, and from the outside, it looked like such an easy job. Even though he always supported that, he never was fully able to appreciate my job and the responsibility of being a stay-at-home mom. That is, until he had all the responsibilities fall on his shoulders. It was a big help when the volunteers came, as my husband needed some time and space for himself. My kids would do homework with the volunteers, eat supper, get ready for bed, and have some time to play. My husband would come home, put the kids to bed, and get ready to go to bed himself.

Thursday was another long day spent in the hospital. Between Shalva recovering from the procedure, waking up from anesthesia, and the ongoing drama. It was the drama that caused me lots of trauma.

That night, I spoke with my sister. I told her I still hadn't made any Shabbos arrangements for my children. Right away, she offered to have all my kids. I really appreciated that, though before confirming anything with her, I told her I had to talk to my husband. I had to make sure he didn't end up making any plans and see if he was up to travel to be with me for Shabbos, or if he wants to be home with the kids.

I spoke to him, and he said he'd do whatever I wanted. On one hand, I wanted him here with me and Shalva, and on the other hand, I wanted him to be with the children at home. I was contemplating and thinking about it. He told me to let him know.

I called my sister back, thanking her for the offer and shared my feelings. I wasn't sure what I wanted to do. She wanted me to be happy, and to be there for me. She said she didn't want me to feel any pressure. Although, the sooner I gave her an answer, the more she'd appreciate it so she could start shopping and cooking.

That night, I was so tired, and I told her I couldn't think straight. She said she'd go shopping, and I should let her know first thing in the morning. I put Shalva to bed early, and I tried to sleep as well. I had a hard time sleeping as I was flooded with emotions.

Early in the morning, my children called me to say hello, check in on Shalva, and see what their Shabbos plans were. I told my kids that before making plans I have to discuss it with Daddy. I then spoke to my husband and told him my sister went shopping last night and would love to have our children over for Shabbos. I put the decision in his hands.

Without thinking twice, he said, "I'm going to pack up the kids, and as soon as they get home from school, I'll drive them over to your sister. I'll then make my way straight to Boston." I gave him a list of things to pack up for me and Shalva. Then my kids came back on the phone, and I told them they were going to my sister, they were really excited.

I quickly called my sister, hoping she was still up for her offer. She sounded so happy and excited to be able to be there for me. It was such a great feeling knowing my kids would be in great hands and they'd have a great experience.

In the meantime, they took Shalva's vitals and blood work and got her ready for the third round of the Sclerotherapy treatment. As it was time, we made our way back to the waiting area with the same protocols as the other days.

Being that it was Friday, as soon as they took her into the OR, I decided to run and take a quick shower as I wanted to make sure I'd have time to shower before Shabbos started. Then I hurried and got dressed. I went back down to the waiting area, and davened until I was called to go to Shalva in the recovery room.

CHAPTER: 22

After the procedure was over, the IR spoke with me and said that it went well. They want to keep her monitored for a couple of days to see how she progresses. He said he'd come back later in the day to speak to me in more depth.

After Shalva woke up in the recovery room, we came back to her room. A short time after, she fell back asleep, and the doctor and Nurse Practitioner (NP) from the Vascular Anomalies team came to introduce themselves. They spoke to me in depth, explaining everything that's going on with Shalva. I asked if I could record the conversation. This way I'll have it for my own personal future reference, and I can share it with my husband as they'll explain it a lot better than I would. They happily agreed to that.

They sat with me for about forty-five minutes explaining what was going on with Shalva. And how there's a certain medication that was just recently approved that they started treating patients with lymphatic malformation with. I was very hesitant as it was a very new medicine. I asked them lots of questions. They said after this conversation is over, the NP will print out the list of benefits and side effects for me to look over.

When the meeting was over, I thanked them, and the NP said she'd be back shortly. Within an hour, she was back in my room. We sat down on the chairs by the table, and she started going over the entire list of risks, side effects, and benefits of Sirolimus. She started off by explaining the benefits of it. It's given to patients who have tumors to prevent them from growing larger. It's supposed to deflate and shrink it.

We were going through the list, and I was getting extremely emotional. The risks and side effects are super scary, though she explained that every medication has lists of scary side effects. Though the benefits outweigh the risks. She told me the most common side effects to look out for and said I should think about them. After sitting with me for forty-five minutes I thanked her so much for all the time she devoted to me, and I said I'd discuss it with my husband and think about it.

My husband called to say that he dropped off the children and he was on his way, I told him I had a lot to discuss with him, and decisions have to be made, so we'll sit down and discuss it when he arrives as I also wanted him to hear the recording before telling him anything.

I was very hesitant, scared, and worried about giving my daughter such a strong medicine. In general, I'm not one that runs to medicine, I'll only take Tylenol if I'm really not functioning, and I'll push myself without it until I get to that point. At the same time, this is my daughter. I don't want to put any toxins and poison in her body, and I don't want her to be in pain and keep on having scares and emergencies.

I kept thinking about it, and I was very torn apart. In the midst of my thoughts, I got a call from my parents and discussed it with them, I told them all my concerns, fears, benefits, and risks. My father suggested that I speak with a close friend of his who's an infectious disease doctor.

I didn't really have the headspace to explain everything again, so my father said he'd call his friend to tell him what I told him, and then I could speak with him after, so that's what I did.

I spoke with him, he was very insightful, sensitive, and thought out. As he walked me through it, he explained to me that, being that Shalva is facing all these scary emergencies, if the doctors are recommending it, it may be beneficial to give it a trial. I was very concerned, but he was extremely understanding and had so much patience and helped me make sense of it.

Before hanging up, he told me that I should feel free to contact him at any time with any questions or concerns. I was very grateful!

As every resident, doctor, and nurse came in to check on Shalva, I asked them their opinion on the medication and what they would do if Shalva was their daughter. I got lots of different feedback. Some said if there's a medication for it, they wouldn't think twice. Some said they would've wanted to start it right away at birth. Some said it's risky and scary, so they don't know what they'd do. Some said they would use it only as a last resort. Others said what's the question, of course they would as it's a gift from G-D. Another one said it's hard to answer as they're not in my shoes. Others said they'd really think it through and get advice, while others said it doesn't hurt to give it a try.

I appreciated everyone's honesty and feedback. On the one hand, I was scared of all the risks. On the other hand, if this would give her a better life as I want the best for her, I'd want her to have that grand opportunity.

In the meantime, I spoke with my sister to check in on how my children were doing. She has a dog, and she said when the children came over, two of them were afraid. She kept the dog away from them, but, as time went on those kids warmed up to the dog. They even started to pet it. I was very impressed and happy to hear they overcame their fear in a safe and healthy environment. My children played with theirs, and they were behaving really well. I spoke to them all, and they were having the time of their lives.

As I hung up with her, I got a call from a sister-in-law to discuss schools for my daughter. She told me she is strongly advocating for her and trying with all her resources and pull to get her into a school. She needed some more information about my daughter, so I told her everything she had to know. She asked me my opinion on something, and wanted to know if I'd be open to changing my mind if the school would require me to. This was a strong value that I wouldn't let down on, and I told her I'd be flexible with other things, though this specific thing I wouldn't. It was a deep, intense conversation, and she wanted me to think it through, though I told her this is something that I'm confident with and not able to budge on. She understood that and hoped no school would require this.

Shortly after, my husband arrived at the hospital. It was close to Shabbos, so he quickly brought in all our belongings and food and put everything away nicely and neatly so we could have a clean room for Shabbos.

When he was settled, I sat down with him. I really wanted him to listen to the recording, though there was no time, so I summarized everything for him. Then I spoke to him about the medicine. Before I even had a chance to tell him any benefits or risks, he said if there's medicine, there's nothing to discuss we are giving it to her.

I then went on to tell him the benefits, and as I was saying them, he was confident as he went on to say this is such a blessing and gift from G-D. He looked at me surprised and asked why I looked so not at ease. I continued by telling him about my forty-five-minute sit down discussion that I had with the Nurse Practitioner, what my father's friend, the infectious disease doctor said, and what all the residents, nurses, and doctors said.

As I was speaking, he kept on saying let's go, let's not waste another moment. Let's start with the medicine right away without delay. I told him my concerns and fears, and he said it wouldn't be fair to Shalva if I don't give her this opportunity because of my worries and fears. As the doctors all said, the benefits outweigh the risks tremendously.

I was still not at ease and felt very unsure, though my husband was very enthusiastic about this. My husband said let's give it a try if it doesn't work, at least we know we tried. If we don't try, this can be a regret we live with for the rest of our lives. It would only be right to give Shalva an opportunity to keep her well and out of pain and suffering.

I still wasn't feeling it and wasn't comfortable. I was very emotional about it; it was a very sensitive subject. I told my husband I was going to daven to Hashem that this should be the right decision as I would agree to start off with it as a trial.

My husband felt so happy and relieved that I was willing to give it a shot. My husband was nervous I'd change my mind, so he quickly called the nurse in to send a message to the doctors that we agreed to start the medicine. He said we would like to begin it right away.

Within an hour, the doctors were back in our room. They told everything to my husband, and he asked some questions. Then he told them before I back out, let's start with the first dosage. They agreed and sent in the scripts.

It was a few minutes to Shabbos, and my husband said we should take a walk around the unit to refresh my mind. I asked our nurse if she could stay with Shalva for a few minutes while we went for a walk, and she was very happy to be there with her.

We went around the unit one time. When we were right outside Shalva's room, the IR came to check in with Shalva and speak with us. He told us that, as of now, they're happy with the results of the procedure. He started telling us plans for the future. He said after Shalva would be discharged, every nine to twelve weeks, he'd like Shalva to come in to get a procedure similar to Sclerotherapy. The only difference is that they would only do it one time, and they would not keep in any drains. She would come in as an outpatient and get to go home the same day. He said he'd like to do this a couple of times, see how it goes and then will see from there how to proceed.

After speaking with the IR, there was a certain sense of relief that we both experienced. There was finally a game plan and hopefully this was a new beginning to a journey of health and healing. This is a peaceful and serene way to enter into Shabbos.

I quickly called to wish my children a good Shabbos and told them how much I miss them and can't stop thinking of them. My daughter was so excited to tell me that since I'm not with her, she is going to light the Shabbos candles. She felt so mature, responsible, and good about herself. I was so happy she had that opportunity. It gave her such a boost of confidence. This moment was one of which she'll never forget.

As I brought in Shabbos, my husband davened in our room and sang the tunes of the Kabbalas Shabbos (it's a prayer that we say that creates joy and peace as we enter into Shabbos) out loud. As he continued singing, the tunes touched my soul and were very uplifting. I just sat down and took in the moment.

He finished his prayers, and we had a nice small meal in the room together. He sang some zemiros to keep the Shabbos spirit alive, and during the meal, we tried to just enjoy the moment and what Shabbos is about. We concluded the meal with benching (the after meal grace).

Just after the meal a resident came in and said they had the medicine and if it's okay with us, they'd give it to her now. My husband right away said yes please let's get it started. They warned us that it tastes really horrible. They mixed it with cherry flavor and had an apple juice box drink for her to wash it down with. She did not like it though she took it really well. They reminded us that it can only go into Shalva's mouth and it's not safe for anyone else to have any of it. If any falls out onto my hand, I should immediately wash it as it shouldn't end up in mine or anyone else's mouth.

In the hospital they'd be giving the medication and upon discharge she suggested that it's not necessary, though if I'd feel more comfortable, I can apply gloves on my hands when I give her the medicine. I was also reminded that this medication is an immune suppressant and that she should avoid direct sunlight as much as possible. There's one food that is counterproductive to this medicine and as long as she's on the medicine, she should not eat any grapefruit. It's not an allergy so she can be in contact and smell it. She just should make sure to avoid eating it or anything that has grapefruit in the ingredients.

We listened carefully to everything that was told to us, and this just made me feel more and more uncomfortable with the medication. The thought that the natural sunlight that's filled with natural vitamin D, which is G-D's creation to bring light onto the world, is no good for my daughter didn't sit well with me. Though, I still said I'd give it a try. I'm going to be keeping my word.

When they left the room, I broke down in tears crying out to Hashem. I know this medication has lots of risks and ingredients I would never want in my body. It's heartbreaking that I'm allowing it in my daughters, please Hashem, let this medication be of only benefit to Shalva and she should not have any side effects. Especially not any scary, dangerous, life-threatening ones.

My husband gave me some time and space and offered to speak. I told him let's call it a night and get some rest as I was very emotional and had a very sleepless, overwhelming week. Within minutes, my husband was out cold for the night, and I was twisting and turning. I couldn't find a comfortable position to sleep in being that I was pregnant, and my mind was full of thoughts and concerns.

Shalva was sleeping, and the doctors and nurses checked on her and did her vitals. I knew now was my chance to get some sleep before the next rounds of vitals were done. I tried to relax my mind and did some self-talk. I told myself Shabbos is a day of peace and rest, and the merit of Shabbos should be a source of healing for Shalva.

Shabbos is a holy and joyous day to connect with Hashem through spirituality. I took some time and talked to Hashem as He is my Father, my King. And He is the only one who has all the answers and can cure and heal Shalva. As I was talking, I found myself relaxed, and at ease. I felt Hashem's presence with me. As I felt relaxed, I fell asleep.

CHAPTER: 23

The morning came, and Shalva slept well through the night. They came in to do her vitals and, shortly after, to give her medicine. My husband finished davening and was learning his daf (page of the Talmud) as they were about to give Shalva her medicine. I was drinking ginger ale and Shalva wanted, so the nurse went to get her a ginger ale can to drink along with the medicine.

She gulped down her medicine as she was excited to drink her ginger ale. When she finished her dose, she gave a face that of how awful the medicine tasted. She then drank her ginger ale. Leaving aside some for later, she placed her drink next to mine.

We spoke to the nurse a little, and then I took a sip to drink. I had an awfully gross taste in my mouth, and naturally, I made a face. The nurse asked what happened. I said I just took a sip to drink, and it must've been from Shalvas can cause I got the most nasty taste in my mouth. She told me to quickly spit everything out and wash out my mouth. She said hopefully, I got it all out.

I davened that I did and that it shouldn't have any effect on me or my baby. She said if I start feeling anything, I should let them know immediately. It was very frightening, though, she said being that it was leftovers from her mouth, and I spat it out right away and washed up, she was not too nervous. However, in the future, I should be more cautious not to have her germs near anyone as soon as she takes her medicine. Being that I tasted it, my heart really went out to her every time she had to have the medicine.

They said within three days from when she starts the medicine, we would see if her body is taking it well, based on symptoms and reactions. So they'd keep her monitored. Over the weekends in the hospital, the surgeons aren't in, and they have different doctors and staff. They said all they see over the weekend will be reported to her doctors and surgeons by Monday when they come back.

Shabbos was over late, and my husband packed up his things and headed out right after he made Havdalah (Blessing that separates the holy Shabbos to the weekday). I called my sister right after Havdalah to see how my children were doing. I let her know that my husband was on the way.

The kids had an amazing Shabbos. My daughter was going to stay with my sister overnight and head to another sister of mine in the morning. My husband went to pick up our sons as they had school the next day. It was really late when my husband picked up my children. He took them straight home to sleep.

In the morning, I spoke to my daughter. She told me all about her Shabbos and how much fun she had. She asked how Shalva was doing and when I was coming home with her. It was very hard for her that I was away. She was going to spend the day with another sister of mine.

The rest of the day I spent at Shalva's side. At the same time, I was still trying to get my daughter in school and dealing with the drama that wouldn't stop as Shalva was just being monitored.

Monday, the doctors came in and said they wanted to do some imaging and some more blood work to see how she was doing and if there were any changes or progress. They said it seems like the medication is doing well with Shalva as she didn't have any negative reactions.

Later on in the day, after the imaging and blood work were done and the results came back, the doctors came in to speak with me. They said that based on how Shalva is doing, they are ready to discharge her as early as tomorrow so long as nothing happens from now until then. And as long as I feel safe going home with her. They said they want me to feel safe and confident before having her discharged.

They prepped me with everything I had to look out for with her and told me not to be hesitant to call or email them at any time. I said at this point, being that she seemed to be doing better, and they came up with a game plan, I was nervous, though I felt ready to go home.

After they left the room, I called my husband to update him with the plans that I'd be discharged at some point tomorrow as long as nothing happens. We should all continue davening for her. He was very excited about the great news. He was contemplating back and forth whether he should stay home with the kids for the night and come to me first thing in the morning or if he should bring my kids over to my sister-in-law. He made a decision that he wanted to come and stay with me overnight, this way we would be ready to go as soon as she is discharged. I told him it's a long travel, so whatever he'd prefer. He thought about it for a moment and then said he would come and stay with us for the night, so he would get some sleep in before he had to drive us all back. This way we will be able to leave immediately without delay as soon as Shalva is discharged.

We ended the conversation with me saying I'd try to make arrangements for my children. My daughter was at my sister's, and I had to figure out arrangements with my three sons. I spoke with my sister-in-law, and we worked it out that my boys would sleep over by them that night and the next day. They would go home straight from school and a volunteer would be there. I called a neighbor to see if their daughter was available to babysit if I wouldn't be back on time when the volunteer would have to leave.

Now I had everything planned out, thanks to Chai Lifeline and all our wonderful family members and neighbors! I called my husband to tell him, and he was very excited about the news. He got the kids bathed and ready for bed in pajamas. He packed them up for the next morning and packed a little bag for himself. He then dropped off the children and made his way towards Boston.

By the time he arrived he was extremely exhausted and went straight to sleep. In the morning, they came into check up on Shalva and said the great news was that we would be discharged. We were very excited about it.

I packed up all our belongings, returned the hospital toys, and cleaned up our room as we waited to be discharged. Shalva was so excited to go back home and see all her siblings that she missed so much.

Finally, we were discharged. We thanked all the doctors and nurses, and they gave us very clear instructions along with the discharge papers. I asked them some more questions and thanked them again as we headed towards the parking lot.

As we got in the parking lot Shalva looked so confused. I told her we were in the parking lot to find our car. She was so excited she said, "Yay, we're going home!" As she started chanting Baruch Hashem! Chasdei Hashem! Todah Hashem (Thank you, Hashem)! No more booboos, and we were going home. She sang that chant with such excitement over and over again.

We got in the car, knowing that it was a long journey home. We decided to go to a kosher restaurant nearby to get some food to eat on the way, and that's what we did.

We then headed towards New York to pick up my daughter. She was so excited to hear that we were coming home, and she couldn't wait to see us! Especially to see Shalva. Shalva was still in pain, so on our journey, we stopped off at a store to buy children's Tylenol for her, and we gave her the proper dose.

We made a few stops on the way and by the time we got to New York, it was already dinner time. We picked up some Chinese food from a restaurant, ate it, then headed straight to my daughter. Her face lit up when she saw us all.

She quickly came running to the car to give Shalva a nice, big, warm hug and kiss. They both were glowing with happiness to see each other.

My daughter quickly gathered her clothing and prizes as we thanked my sister for watching her and giving her so much TLC. We hugged and said goodbye. We then ran over to my parents house for a few minutes just so they could see Shalva. When I was there, I spoke with my sister, and I told her I'd stop by her house on the way home.

It was about a forty-five-minute car ride to my sister's house. The whole car ride, my daughter was telling us everything she's done, how much fun she had, and how homesick she was. She shared her excitement about seeing Shalva and that we were all finally going home.

It started to rain outside, so my husband said I should run in with Shalva and my other daughter while he looks for parking, so we don't have to get so wet. We quickly ran into the house. I was holding Shalva, and I said I can't believe how wet her dress got. I was literally outside in the rain for less than a minute. I looked at my hand, and I noticed blood. I looked at her dress and noticed more blood, which got me frightened. I tried to be in denial and said maybe my hand was bleeding I looked, and all I saw was dry blood. I picked up her dress and noticed the blood was leaking through the gauze that was on her stomach.

I quickly called my husband, and he said he had just found a parking spot, he was coming in. I told him to run, he asked if everything was okay, and I burst out crying. I said, "come in quick; she's bleeding." He sounded nervous and asked, "who, Shalva? Where? What?!" I was hysterically crying. I said, "I can't speak. Come in quick and you'll see!"

He ran into the house and saw the blood. He told me to call the doctors immediately, but I was way too emotional to speak. I got him the number to the emergency hotline of the doctors. He left a message and then called the man who helped us get to Boston in the first place. He updated him on the situation, and he said we should go immediately back to Boston. He said he would try to help us get a helicopter ride there so we can get there sooner.

My husband thanked him and said the doctor was calling in on the other line, so he'd call him back right after he spoke with them. My husband hung up quickly and answered the call. It was a resident on call. My husband gave him a brief rundown that we had just been discharged midafternoon and that we had just seen the blood. He asked him some questions and said he'd speak to the team and get back to us.

I was nervous, worried, scared, and emotional. The food didn't sit well with me, and it caused me to have a stomachache. My husband called the man back and said before we arrange for any helicopter, let's just wait and see what they tell us when they call us back.

I wasn't up to talking, though I pushed myself to call my sister-in-law to give her brief updates and asked her to take my children for the night and send the babysitter home. She was very nervous; I just couldn't talk. I told her to just daven and Im Yirtza Hashem (G-d willing), everything would be good.

After a while of waiting, it was about half an hour, the resident called back and asked if it had stopped bleeding. As soon as we told him it was actively bleeding, he said we should go to the hospital. He wasn't sure if it was safe for us to wait to get all the way back to Boston, so he said he'd get back to us.

My daughter was hysterical, she was so scared and felt so let down. We were psyched up and excited to go home as a family, and now we told her we were heading back to the hospital, and she would be going back to my sister's house. She was devastated and emotional. I gave her a huge hug and kiss and tried explaining to her that, unfortunately, we had an emergency and let's daven that Im Yirtza Hashem (G-d willing) Shalva should be healthy, well, and okay. I told her I'd be in touch with her and that when she gets back to my sister's house, she should call me so I can say good night to her.

Feeling very weak emotionally and physically, I thanked my sister, and we headed straight towards the car. We started driving as we didn't want any time to be wasted. About an hour later, the resident called back and asked where we were. We said we started driving and were on the road. They said they were nervous for us to go all the way to Boston with her actively bleeding. We should rather go to a nearby hospital.

We looked in the GPS, and we were about a twenty-five-minute drive to Yale Hospital in Connecticut. We headed towards there as my husband called the man to update him. I sat in the back next to Shalva the entire time making sure she was alert, checking in on her coloring, and keeping a very close eye on her as I recited some Tehillim. We got to the hospital and checked in. As soon as we said she was bleeding, they took us in right away. They said we would continue to fill out forms in the room as she's being seen.

They took us to a room in the ER, and we briefly gave them a rundown of her medical history. They did blood work right away. I told them that she had hard veins to find, and it's been working out with the ultrasound, so they quickly got the ultrasound to take some blood work.

As they did the blood work she was snuggled into me, as my husband held her hand, trying to distract her, and a nurse turned on a video. I davened that they should find a good vein and get the blood they needed right away and Baruch Hashem that's what happened.

Shortly after, they came in to do an abdominal ultrasound. As they asked us more questions, they said they didn't have experience with this and that they would wait for the bloodwork to come back. In the meantime, they finished up with weighing her and getting her height and had me fill out some forms.

They came back and showed us her blood work, and it pretty much matched the numbers that we left Boston. They said it's better for us to go back to Boston, where the doctors are familiar with the case. They discharged us on the condition we head straight to Boston, so that's what we did.

CHAPTER: 24

Before discharging Shalva, they wrapped a dressing around the bleeding and gave us some extra gauze and dressing to take with us if need be. We then thanked them and continued on our journey.

My parents were nervous and couldn't sleep. They kept calling to check on Shalva and how we were doing. I updated them and told them to just daven and go to sleep, and I'd call or text them if there's any major updates.

We packed back into our car and headed towards Boston which was another three-hour drive. It was a long, tiring, and emotional day. We had time to discuss our feelings, fears, and emotions. On the way, my husband got a blasting headache from his lack of sleep, emotions, and traveling. We stopped off at a CVS to buy Tylenol. I waited in the car with Shalva as my husband ran in.

We then continued on to Boston. It was about 5:00 a.m. when we finally arrived. We weren't sure if we would be admitted or not, and how long the stay was going to be. So, we took Shalva's carriage in with some food and drinks.

We ran into the hospital and signed in right away. They asked us what we were here for, and we told them briefly. They checked her vitals and sent us immediately into the Emergency Room.

We got into a unit in the ER, and the nurse asked us some questions. They ordered blood work and an ultrasound. Within a few minutes, they came in to do the blood work. My heart poured out for Shalva. She's been through so much, and every blood test is another prick of more pain. I tried to keep Shalva calm and told her hopefully, after this blood test, she wouldn't need to be pricked anymore. She was not taking to this well, though I explained to her it's important for the doctors to see what's going on with your blood work. I reassured her that both me and Daddy would be with her the entire time. She snuggled into me as my husband tried holding her hand, and the nurses showed her a video. I said some Tehillim as they were giving her a blood test. I was talking to Hashem in my own words, asking that everything should be okay, and her blood results should come back well.

A short while later, they came in to do an ultrasound exam. After doing it, they said they would review it and discuss it with the IR (Interventional Radiologist) to see what was going on and how to proceed. They told me that someone from the IR team would come to check on Shalva after they reviewed the exam.

In the meantime, the blood work came back, and Chasdei Hashem the hemoglobin numbers came back good, as well as the other numbers.

We waited for a while until the Nurse Practitioner from the IR came to check in on Shalva. After examining Shalva, she told us that her team reviewed the ultrasound, and now, after examining her, it's confirmed what happened. After the drains were taken out from Sclerotherapy, the skin was glued closed and left for healing.

The glue did not hold properly, which caused leakage from her procedure. They said Thank G-D, it's a real quick fix. All that has to be done is it has to be reglued together again.

Baruch Hashem, we felt such a huge sense of relief. We felt such excitement and happiness knowing that she was okay. We were extremely thankful.

At this point, we were so excited yet super tired and knew we had a long journey ahead of us. We decided that until they came back to the room to glue her and dress the wound, to get some sleep. We shut the lights and closed our eyes for a little sleep.

Shalva had other plans. She had no intentions of sleeping and was as awake as can be. I took her into the hallway and walked around with her a bit as my husband took a small nap on the ER bed.

Going back a couple of hours earlier, as we arrived at the ER, the dashboard light came up. We were scared to drive all the way back without getting it checked out at the mechanic. As he woke up from his nap, my husband found a nearby mechanic. As we were waiting for Shalva to be reglued, the mechanic took a quick look before our long five hour journey home.

Thank G-D, the mechanic was able to get the car up and running within a very short time frame. My husband then ran to get some kosher bagels and sweatshirts as it was getting cold, and we were not properly prepared for this weather.

He got back perfect timing as they were gluing Shalva and getting the discharge papers ready. That process was surprisingly very quick. All we wanted was to go home and reunite with our family, and we all needed a break from the hospital and a good night's sleep. Within a few minutes, we thanked the doctors and headed towards the parking lot with exhaustion, overtiredness, and excitement. We were so grateful and thankful to Hashem. We all had a sense of relief, with hope and Emunah (belief in G-d) that we would be home from the hospital with a nice break up until the next scheduled appointment.

As we entered the car and started our journey, Shalva was so happy that we were going home. Her face lit up with so much joy. I told her we were all going to continue to daven for her, that she would continue to heal and get better and that there would be no more emergencies.

It was lots and lots of traveling. Shalva and I both fell asleep, I dozed off for a little bit, and Shalva took a long awaited nap.

We got to New York to pick up my daughter. She was so excited to see us, though she feared the same thing would happen again. I explained to her that the booboo was leaking, and they had to reglue it back together. We should continue to daven for Shalva's health and wellbeing and no more emergencies.

She had lots of questions, and we always made sure to give her and all our children a safe place to feel comfortable and ask questions. Patiently, on our way home, I listened and answered all her questions. While answering, I added a strong sense of Emunah and that Hashem is in control and He is the Ultimate One, the Healer. We have a great power, that power is, the power of Tefillah (prayer) and that can change decrees.

After speaking with her, the nervous, worried look on her face turned a lot more calm and serene. She actually felt that she could help, which is 100% true as every Tefillah helps.

We picked up the boys and headed straight home. It was already late at night. They were all tired and exhausted and they were so excited to see Shalva and be back home with us. They kissed and hugged her up gently, spoke to her, and went to bed.

It was really cute to see how sensitive my children were to Shalva. They were all super overprotective of her. They all have such a strong sense of pride and felt privileged to have such a miraculous sister with such a holy neshama (soul).

In the days following, when we got home, the kids were overflowing with joy. When they looked at Shalva, their faces lit up and glowed. It was so beautiful for me to see and it gave me such strength.

For the next few days, we had to change the dressing and keep it from being exposed to getting wet. During this time, I gave her hand baths. I watched over her very cautiously, and I told my children that we had to make sure to keep Shalva safe. Nothing and no one should bump into her, and we should watch out for falls.

My kids were very helpful. They were super cautious over her and made sure when they played alongside her, to be very calm and gentle. They kept on asking her how she felt and how her booboo was doing. Now that we were home, I had to give her the medication twice a day. It was not an easy task as it tasted so horrible. I bought her cherry flavor to mix in with it. That didn't help. I tried mixing it with different juices, but she did not like it. Every time I had to give her it, it tore my heart apart.

After a while, I told her if she took it nicely, I'd give her a treat. She asked for ice cream, and so after her dose of medicine was followed with a spoonful of ice cream. This lasted for quite some time until she got used to taking it.

I explained to her as gross as it tastes, I don't want to see her suffer even a tiny more. The only reason I'm giving this medicine to her is for it to hopefully help make her booboo get better. As she started to understand, that helped her take it quickly, easily, and nicely. As she just wanted the booboo to go away.

Over the next couple of weeks, we tried our best to stay strong and tried to keep her from being exposed to anyone sick, as the medication she was on lowered her immune system. Any time any of us would get sick, I'd call her doctor immediately. Sometimes, we were told to stop with the medication until everyone was feeling better. Other times, they said to keep a close eye on her as long as she shows no signs of symptoms she can continue. If she has any symptoms, we should stop the medication immediately.

This was not an easy task, though we did all it took, as all we wanted was the best for our precious princess! She knew and felt that we all had her best interest. And most importantly, we showered her with an abundance of love and compassion at all times!

About two weeks later, we had a follow up with the team of doctors. We made arrangements for the kids when they got back home from school with a Chai Lifeline girl to watch them. If we were not home on time, we arranged for a babysitter to be there until we got home.

Telling my children the plans caused lots of mixed feelings and emotions. Some of my kids were scared, others were nervous, and some were really worried. They were all scared we would go and stay for a while. They finally felt adjusted and united together as a family. They didn't want to lose those moments and they didn't want Shalva to be admitted.

I told them that based on how Shalva seems to be doing, let's all daven, I reassured them that I'm not worried. The doctors just want to check up on her, do some blood work, and we will G-D willingly be back home the same day. I told them if there were any changes, I'd let them know right away. However, I was pretty confident that it was just a regular follow up appointment.

After dropping the children off at my sister-in-law bright and early in the morning to have her bring my boys to the bus and my other son to school, we headed towards the hospital for Shalva's follow up. We met some more doctors, and they were happy with the progress so far. Yet, it was still premature to really know how successful it may be. Being that she didn't have any side effects, they felt very hopeful with this medication.

Before being seen by the doctors, Shalva had her blood taken to see the medication level in her blood. Since it was a very strong medication, they had to monitor her blood very closely. She was scared and didn't want the blood test. We explained to her why it was important and needed and told her that as soon as she was finished with the bloodwork, she could eat. We were informed she shouldn't eat anything for three hours prior to the blood test. She was hungry, so she cooperated nicely to get it done.

During the appointment, they went more into detail again explaining how the medication works and how it should help shrink the LM (Lymphatic Malformation). They answered all of our questions, gave us lots of support and encouragement with our concerns, and reassured us even though we were a long drive away. We are just a phone call and an email away. I should never hesitate to call with any questions, comments, or concerns and that was very reassuring.

Baruch Hashem, her blood levels looked good, her vitals were all good, and Shalva did great through her exam. We were good to go back home. She was so excited to go home. As we left the hospital, she had a huge smile that was glued to her face!

CHAPTER: 25

Driving was very exhausting, especially for so many hours. Our travel started after 7:30 a.m. after my husband came home from davening Shachris (Morning prayers). On the way to the hospital, we got gas and drove straight. On the way back, we made a few stops for coffee, bathroom breaks, and to fill up on gas.

We got home exhausted after a long day of traveling. Chai Lifeline provided supper, which was a massive help as I had no energy to think of making dinner after such a long day. My kids were so excited to see us as we entered through the doors. It was the cutest when one of my children said, "I knew Shalva was coming home because we all davened for her."

They ran straight to Shalva and greeted her with hugs and kisses. And signs that they made her, and showed her others that they hung in her room. The joy and happiness showered the air.

By the time we got home, they had all eaten, showered, were in pajamas, and ready for bed. They all gathered together as they asked me every detail about our day. The traveling, how long did it take? Was there traffic? Did we make it to the appointments on time? What did Shalva do right away when we got to the hospital? Did she get a blood test? Did she cry? What did the doctors do to her? What did they say? And many more questions. I answered all their questions. It's very important that they felt very part of Shalva's entire journey.

I walked them each to their own bed, said Shema with them, gave them all a hug and kissed them all good night, and reminded them how Hashem loves hearing our tefillos. Especially from young children, as they each have such a pure and holy neshama (soul). After my kids went to bed, I showered and went straight to sleep.

The next couple of weeks, we all continued with our regular everyday routines and kept a close eye on Shalva. Baruch Hashem, there was nothing alarming or concerning.

We scheduled a procedure as an outpatient before being discharged from the hospital. As time moved on, the appointment was nearing. We got a call that due to the spike of coronavirus; she will have to have a COVID PCR test in their facility within thirty-six hours before the procedure. With that being the case, I scheduled it for around 4:30 p.m. the day before the procedure.

As the day of the appointment was nearing, we arranged for my kids to go straight from school to my sister-in-law and sleep there overnight. The next day, a Chai Lifeline volunteer would be at the house. If we wouldn't be home on time we had a babysitter on call.

I didn't tell my kids until the day before as I didn't want them to have too much time to think and worry about it. I informed the school and all their teachers. This way my kids would get the extra support they may need.

My kids were nervous when I told them, though I explained to them very gently that this was planned. It's the process of helping Shalva get better. They had lots of questions. I answered some and told them I'd have more answers after the procedure was over.

I took them to the bus stop early in the morning and reminded them that they would be going straight to my sister-in-law after school. I told them I would miss them and love them so much and was sad to leave them. Though before they knew it, we would be back home.

After getting everyone to school, we dropped my daughter off by my sister-in-law and started our travel to Boston. On the way, we booked a nearby hotel as we had to stay overnight. We went to the hospital to get Covid tested, and then we went to a kosher restaurant to eat dinner and made our way to the hotel. I made sure Shalva ate really well, as she couldn't eat past midnight due to her procedure the next morning.

The next morning, we woke up bright and early. I bathed Shalva as my husband davened Shachris. When I was done, I got a phone call. I kept on receiving emails from Norton that I had a balance, and since it's not being paid on time the balance keeps on rising. I spoke to them and told them I didn't have a computer and I never used Norton that they must be billing me for the wrong person.

They apologized for the numerous emails and said the only way that they could cancel the charges was if I downloaded an app. Without thinking twice, I did, and the next thing I knew, they had full access to my phone. I got nervous and told them to stop, but they didn't listen.

I tried shutting off my phone, but I had no access until I went into the elevators, where there was no reception. I quickly took advantage of that moment to shut my phone. I kept my phone off for the next couple of hours as I was nervous and felt that I was just phone hacked.

Being that we traveled a lot and slept very little the night before, I was exhausted and nervous about the procedure. I couldn't think twice as I was very vulnerable at that time.

We drove to the hospital, and on the way, we were trying to brainstorm what to do. Now that someone else has had access to my phone, using my husband's phone I quickly changed the passwords of my accounts that I had on my phone.

That day was very nerve wrecking. After changing passwords, I had to put all this aside as I had to tend and be fully present for Shalva to give her all the care she needs. My husband and I decided we will not discuss this until we're out of the hospital.

It was a very long day. We got to the hospital early in the morning, and Shalva was nervous as she knew that she was going in for a procedure. I calmed her by telling her the doctor was going to put her to sleep. While she was sleeping, Hashem would help the doctor get rid of some of her booboo. She remembered from previous surgeries and procedures that after it's done, she wakes up feeling very oozy and dizzy and out of it.

I comforted her, telling her I would wait with her until she went into the OR. I'd be davening to Hashem and my husband would be learning, and it should be a zechus (merit) for her procedure to go smoothly and well without any complications. The doctors should be the perfect shaliach (messenger), and as soon as she's done the surgery, I would meet her in the recovery room and stay with her the whole time.

When she told me she was hungry, I told her after the procedure, when she wakes up, we would give her food and drinks as soon as she was able to eat and drink. She was uncomfortable being hungry, besides for that, she looked much more at ease, calm, and content.

During the wait, she switched off sitting on my lap and my husband's, and we got to spend lots of quality time with her. At the same time, we kept her distracted from thinking about the procedure.

When she mentioned that she felt scared about the procedure, we validated those feelings and let her speak her feelings out. As it's so important for her to feel heard and understood. We told her how strong she is and how proud we are of her that even though she's been through so much, she sees positivity through everything and always has a beautiful smile glowing on her face.

The time came, and the doctor came with some consent forms for us to sign. He explained to us the procedure is similar to Sclerotherapy, though it's a one-day procedure, not a three-day cycle, and they take the drains out right away. He answered all our questions, and we handed him back the signed consent forms.

A few minutes later, the anesthesiologist team came. They asked us some questions, got some information, and briefly told us what they were going to be doing. We then signed the consent forms as they left.

Moments later, they came to get Shalva to take her to the OR. I went with her and held her hand until they dismissed us. I gave her a kiss, a bracha, said a Perek of Tehillim, and went to wait in the waiting area. The entire time in the waiting area my husband was learning his daf (page of the Talmud) I was saying Tehillim. I had my phone on the ringer right near me as I would be ready to answer as soon as I got the call that the procedure was over.

As soon as my phone rang, I answered. The nurse told us to wait there, and the doctor would come to meet us and take us to the recovery room. They said the procedure went well. I said a little more Tehillim as my husband started wrapping up his thoughts from the Gemara. I then put away my Tehillim as the doctor approached us.

He spoke to us as he walked us to the recovery room, we wanted to get there before she woke up, he told us that the procedure went well, and there was no complications and time will tell if this was successful when the swelling goes down, we will be able to tell if it's a success. Moving forward he would want to do another procedure every nine to twelve weeks for the next couple of months, and then we would reevaluate.

He told us to keep that area dry, and not to let any pressure directly on it, and be more sensitive to that area for some time. He gave us extra dressing so we could keep on changing the gauze. Everyone's healing time is different, so I'll see with Shalva.

In the meantime, refrain from jumping or wild activities, and if there are any concerns or questions, we shouldn't hesitate to call at any time. And just keep a close eye on her for now. We thanked him and went straight to Shalva.

Shalva was crying. I quickly ran to her, and the nurse helped transfer her onto my lap without any monitoring wires falling off. She fell asleep in my arms as I recited some more Tehillim, asking Hashem that it should be a healthy, easy, successful, and speedy recovery. At the same time, my husband continued learning his daf (page of the Talmud).

After a while, being in the recovery room, seeing Shalva in the state she was in, and seeing other patients coming in, I started feeling a bit dizzy. I quickly told my husband, and he got the nurse. Right away they helped me transfer Shalva back into the crib and got me some water and ginger ale and kosher crackers. I drank a bit and put my head down for a few minutes. And Baruch Hashem after some time passed, I started feeling back to myself.

Shalva woke up. I asked her if she wanted to drink, she said yes, and the nurse gave me a bottle and an apple juice box drink. My husband went to rinse the bottle out and then I poured the juice into the bottle and gave it to her.

She drank it nicely and then she was hungry. The nurse gave her a freeze pop and shortly after some crackers. Once they saw she was eating and drinking well, they started working on getting the discharge papers ready.

While we were waiting, I spoke to my sister-in-law and updated her that the procedure went well. I asked her how my daughter was doing, and how she's been.

After about half an hour of waiting, they came back with Shalva's discharge papers. They reviewed it with us thoroughly and told us all the discharge instructions. They told us to give Tylenol around the clock for pain as needed. She still had some painkillers in her system and told us to make sure we buy Tylenol before traveling home. This way, Shalva wouldn't need to suffer.

We thanked the nurses and headed straight towards our car. We started driving and remembered there was a pharmacy in the hospital. Though once we left, we didn't want to go back in. We put in the navigation to the closest pharmacy and made our way over. We bought Tylenol and some water for the car ride home.

We then went to a kosher restaurant and got some food. We took it to go and ate in the car. We tried not to make any extra delay. Shalva was sleeping, and we wanted to travel as much as we could before she awoke. Being that she had anesthesia, we wanted her to sleep it off as much as possible so she wouldn't feel oozy and irritable. Also, we knew that as long as she slept, the pain must be bearable. Otherwise, she would wake up from the pain.

We drove for three hours straight when we noticed we needed some gas. As we pulled up to the gas station, Shalva woke up. It was perfect timing. We filled up on gas and parked in the rest area. I took her out of her car seat gently. Then I went outside with her for some fresh air. After about half an hour at the rest stop, I gently put her back in her car seat, and she started to cry. I gave her Tylenol as it was time, and I didn't want her to suffer or be in any extra moment of pain. I then walked around with her outside for a few more minutes until I saw that she seemed happier and more content. I then put her back in the car as we continued the journey home.

We turned on some music to keep her relaxed so that she could fall back asleep. I sat next to her in the back to comfort her. I sang softly to her as she held my hand until she dozed off to sleep.

CHAPTER: 26

After such a long, tiring, exhausting, and emotional day, which started with my phone being hacked, I couldn't see straight anymore. I just needed to sleep, so I closed my eyes and slowly drifted into a light sleep. I took a short nap until my phone rang. It was my parents calling to check in on how Shalva was feeling and doing. I quickly updated them and told them I was too exhausted to speak.

I couldn't fall back asleep. We came straight to my sister-in-law, picked up my daughter and son, and went back home to my other kids. They were there with the Chai Lifeline volunteer. The kids were so excited to see that we really came home. We thanked the volunteer girl as she left the house.

The kids have already eaten supper. We sat down as they needed attention and wanted to know the details of everything. They told me all about their day in school and at home. They each shared their feelings and emotions. Then I answered all their many questions that they had. As bedtime was approaching, I started sending them one by one to take a shower and get into pajamas. When everyone was ready, I said Shema with them and put them to bed.

I took Shalva to my room. My husband watched her as I showered and got ready for bed. I then went straight to sleep. I fell asleep so fast as tiredness has befallen upon me. I woke up throughout the night to tend to Shalva's needs.

The next day, my husband continued his routine of waking up early, learning his daf (page of the Talmud), going to Shul to daven Shacharis, and started his commute to work before any of us woke up.

The alarm went off at 7:15a.m. I woke everyone up and they all washed up and got dressed quietly so as not wake up Shalva. I then served them all breakfast and got them ready for school. We had a few minutes to talk before waiting for the bus to come.

The boys were all in school and I was home with my two girls. My older daughter loved spending quality time with me and Shalva. We had lots of time together and she loved every moment of it. During the day I was still working on making calls to try getting her into a school.

Day after day we were all trying with no success, as she was still not in school. With many people reaching out and advocating there was still no school that would take her in or even interview her. It was really devastating, and heartbreaking.

As time went on it was getting really difficult for her and taking a toll on her. She felt a massive sense of rejection and couldn't understand why no school wanted her. I told her it was nothing personal as they didn't even know her, and they hadn't interviewed or met her. As hard as it was for me, I had to keep on encouraging her.

My son's teacher knew my daughter's situation and was so generous, sweet, and kind. She spoke with me and sent home a whole booklet of schoolwork for her to do to keep her busy and educated. I really appreciated that.

I then decided to make a structured schedule with her every day. She would wake up, get dressed, eat breakfast, then daven, say some Tehillim, read a short book or a chapter of a story, do some math and two work pages from the booklet, and then practice her violin. This way she wouldn't fall behind, and she would feel productive and have a sense of responsibility.

It worked out nicely as she did it, though it was a really sad situation that she wasn't in school. We tried to make the most of it, but it was not an easy time in her life.

In the meantime, we had to be out of our rental in less than two months, and we had nowhere to go. Being that we were back and forth in the hospital, we didn't have the time to be proactive with looking for a house to buy. Now that it was two months away, we started asking around and looking at advertisements for rentals.

My husband spoke to me and said we have to be out of here by January 15, so by the time January 1st arrives, if we don't find a rental to live in, we will have no choice but to rent some storage space for all our belongings. I looked at him and said it was very nice to find a place to lodge our belongings, but what about us? He said we would have no choice but to live with family until we find a rental.

He saw I didn't look thrilled about that idea, and I told him that was not an option, as it had been a very hard year since we moved to New Jersey between Shalva with the hospitals, and my daughter without a school. I said it's important that we find a place to live so that kids can feel settled and at home. He agreed with me about that and said that it is ideal, and that's what we are striving for, but we have to be realistic. If we don't find a place, we can't be homeless.

We both kept davening to Hashem to help us find a rental before January 1st. I was not picky with neighborhoods as I felt desperate. As long as it was in the same township as my boy's school that they could get transportation.

I called all the rentals that had enough bedrooms to fit our family comfortably, which was not many, and scheduled appointments to go check it out. The rental availabilities came in very slowly at this point. It was already mid-December when we made an appointment to go check out a rental home for the next night.

The next day, my husband planned on being home from work on time as we had an appointment to check out the rental and a cousin's engagement party. I hired a babysitter, and all arrangements were made.

At lunch time, I took my older daughter and Shalva to pizza for lunch with my sister-in-law. While we were eating, I got a text message from my phone company with a one-time pin that expires shortly. I quickly called my husband and asked him if he had gone into the phone store or called our phone service company. Confused why I'm asking, he said no, why? I told him that's so strange. I just got a message with a one-time pin, which they text to the phone for security purposes. I told him I'd call to find out what was going on.

I tried to call, but my phone wasn't working. I figured it must be the service. I told my kids to hurry quickly to finish eating so we could leave the store where I'd have reception.

A few minutes later, we all left. I tried calling my husband, but it wasn't going through. I tried calling my sister-in-law, but it wasn't going through. She tried calling me, but it went straight to voice mail. I didn't know what was happening. I tried restarting my phone, and still, the phone was not working. I was not able to make or receive any calls.

I used a different phone line and called our phone service company. I spoke with them and told them that I got a security code at the time I got it, and a few minutes later, my phone didn't work for incoming or outgoing calls. They asked me some security questions, which I answered correctly right away.

They then told me to wait while they checked the system. They told me that at that time, someone came in saying they were me and that their phone was lost or stolen. They bought an iPhone and wanted my SIM card with all the memory on it. So, they gave it to them and that's why my SIM card is not working. They gave me a new one so that I'd be able to use my phone.

They said that the SIM card was already given, and there's no way to retract that. Any messages or calls that came in today went to them. And anything saved to the sim card and phone they may have access to.

They were able to give me a new SIM number attached to my phone so that I'd be able to move forward and use my phone, what was done is done! I thanked them for their time, assistance, and help then I hung up the phone.

I called my husband to update him on the conversation I had with the phone service company. I was nervous, though I said Gam Zu L'Tova (This, too, is for the best). I had to pick up one of my kids from school, so I told my husband we would talk more about this later that day.

I picked up my son from school and tried to give him all the necessary attention that I usually give him when he gets home. Although I was nervous, I said, right now, my job is to be a mommy and take care of my kids. I'll deal with everything later on after my kids are in bed.

I prepared supper, and shortly after my other boys came home from school, I spent some time with them. I spoke to them about their day in school, fed them supper, and did their homework with them. Then it was shower and pajama time, and they had some time to play.

Shortly after my husband got home, he washed up, showered, and got dressed. Then spoke to the kids for a few minutes and put them to bed as I showered and got ready to go. When I was ready, everyone was already in bed. I went to say good night and gave them each a good night hug and kiss.

I then called the babysitter to say that we would be ready to leave in about ten to fifteen minutes. We both quickly finished getting ready, and I tidied up my kitchen. The babysitter came, and we left. We took Shalva along, as I never left her with any babysitter.

When we were in the car, we were talking about what happened with the phone service. Then thinking back, I put two and two together. I remembered how a month earlier when we were about to leave the hotel to go to the hospital for Shalva's procedure, my phone was hacked. This started frightening me. I said if they were able to get into my phone and then get my SIM card, who knows what they can access or have accessed?

Our minds were not in the right setting to check out an apartment. We both took deep breaths and said we were going to check it out and continue talking after. We walked through the apartment. Within five minutes we then thanked them for letting us check it out and hurried back to our car.

We said we would go to the bank to pick up money for the babysitter and then go to the engagement party to wish them a Mazel Tov (Congratulations).

We went to the bank, and I put my card in the ATM machine. It said the card was inactive. I was so confused my husband said maybe I put it in the wrong way. I tried again, and the same thing happened. My card worked earlier when I was in the pizza shop. My husband then tried, and again, it said the card was inactive.

My husband then took his card. It worked, but it showed that we had a balance of $0.00 in our account. We knew something wasn't right as I knew I had money in my account.

I tried logging into my online banking app, and it said it was the wrong password. Now I knew we were hacked and robbed. I was able to change my password to log in, and I saw my checking account had a zero-dollar balance. Lots of hard-earned money was taken out of my savings account. My husband tried withdrawing money from our savings account, though it didn't allow us to, as it reached its maximum number of withdrawals for the day.

I quickly called the bank and started to talk. In the middle of the conversation, they said one moment, and the voice changed to someone with an accent. They were asking me personal questions. My husband told me to hang up immediately, so I did. He told me that before anything, the banks send a security code to verify it's really you, and we didn't get a security code. We tried from his phone, the same story.

We were both nervous and worried. We then went to the engagement party. I quickly said Mazel Tov to everyone, and then I told my mother what happened. I asked her for her phone and ran back to my car. My husband and I called the bank together using my mother's phone, and this time, they sent me the code. We gave them a whole rundown of everything that happened. After verifying it was me with the security code and answering questions, she looked into it. She put us on hold for a couple of minutes.

She came back on the line and asked if any of us went to the bank today to get a replacement card, and we said no. She said that it seemed like someone came into the bank saying they were you and got a replacement card. Meaning, they got a new card with a new number, so this card will not work anymore. They went to a few different ATM machines and took out some cash, and they actually, in person, took out some more money.

We couldn't believe it. Can this be true, did this really happen?! She told us that we should file a police report and go to the bank and file a fraud claim! She told us in the meantime, we should change all our passwords and have the bank put a freeze on our account. She was very helpful, and she apologized that we were hit with this. We were very appreciative and thanked her for all her guidance, advice, and help.

We ran into the engagement party for a few more minutes. I gave my mother back her phone and quickly summed up what had just happened. How my phone was hacked, and we were robbed. She couldn't believe it, she felt so bad and asked tons of questions out of concern. I told her what we were told and then we headed back home.

I don't like owing money, had I known the outcome that we experienced that night, I wouldn't have left my house. Though it was good we did go so I was able to find out about the bank and use my mother's phone to deactivate the thief's replacement cards. I also got to know what steps were needed for us to take moving forward.

We got home and I spoke to the babysitter. I told her briefly that my phone was hacked and robbed, and I had no access to my account and wasn't able to take out any money. I told her I owed her money and that I would try to pay her as soon as possible. I felt really bad and kept apologizing, she was so understanding and felt bad for us. We then thanked her and wished her a good night.

We spoke a lot about what happened together, and it was a massive challenge. Our account was empty, and our life savings were nearly empty, which we had worked really hard and patiently to save up money to try to buy a house. Our house money was almost gone. At this moment, my husband saw lots of time and hard work vanish before his very eyes. It was hard.

When you rob someone, it's like you murdered them. One of the Hebrew words for money is damim, which also means blood. Our hard-working life savings account appeared to be gone in front of our very eyes.

My husband spoke to our Rabbi and told him everything that had just happened. The day before, we gave a very nice donation towards an organization. We didn't question why G-D did this to us right after we gave a large sum of money to tzedakah (charity). The Rabbi explained to my husband it could've been that we deserved a bigger punishment at that moment. It could be that G-D took away our materialistic belongings rather than taking our life or health away from us. We should accept this with love as a gift from Hashem, and it was a chessed (kindness) of Hashem.

Tzedaka Tatzil Mimaves (charity saves from death). We felt so grateful that we gave tzedakah the day before. There's always a reason for everything. When we gave the donation, we didn't think of anything other than we were happy to donate to a wonderful organization. After all this happened, we realized this is what saved us from what could've been a bigger catastrophe.

CHAPTER: 27

After hearing what our Rabbi said, we really appreciated the moment and knew it was there to help us grow closer to Hashem spiritually. Also, this situation brought us close to each other and it strengthened our relationship with each other.

The invoices that we kept on getting were coming through my husband's business email account, which, due to all this, we had to shut his business down. His business got shuttered, and our bank got emptied. On the outside, it looked like a huge disaster had fallen upon us, though it brought us a lot closer to each other.

We knew that this was a test given to us by Hashem, and we both committed to stay strong and pass this test. As with any challenge in life that we are faced with, it's all coming from Hashem, and we don't know why we are being tested. What we do know is that whatever test we are being faced with, is there to make us stronger, better people, and closer to Hashem if we pass the test.

Situations like this can cause a lot of tension and distress between a couple. So, we both decided and made it a priority to use this situation to better ourselves and get closer to each other through this stumbling block.

As hard of a challenge as this was, I was grateful that it was materialistic things taken from us. Even though we were planning on trying to get the money back, it was still a massive test. We were so glad and thankful to Hashem that it wasn't Shalva's health on the line or any of our lives.

It was hard to sleep that night as I was fluttered with many different thoughts and nerves. I said Shema and asked Hashem to help us stay strong and guide us through this whole challenging process.

The next morning, we woke up and got our kids ready for school. I sent my daughter to my sister-in-law, as we went to the precinct to file a police report. We waited outside in the cold until a policeman came and spoke with us. We told him all we knew and gave him all the information he needed.

We then went straight to the phone service store and decided to shut down our phone plans completely. We decided to get a new number and go on a prepaid phone plan for the time being. When that was done, we headed over to the bank.

We waited a couple of minutes until our turn and told them the whole story. I showed them the transaction I made in the pizza shop here in New Jersey, and they saw the ATM transaction was in Pennsylvania only a few minutes after I made my purchase.

They couldn't believe how they went to the bank and got a replacement card under my name. They filled out a withdrawal slip, and the bank manager showed it to us. Being that it was during COVID, and it was cold out they were probably wearing hoods and masks which made it hard to identify them. Though they said they would do further research to get footage and more investigation with the actual bank they went into.

They asked us many questions. As we were making a fraudulent claim, we signed forms. We kept our account frozen until this would be settled, and they will try their best to get us back the money. It will be a very long and excruciating process. In essence, the bank was telling us to put on our seat belts as you're in for a long ride. Just try to stay calm and patient. Our family learned to adapt to our new reality and move forward with our lives.

As the days went by, it was getting closer and closer to January. We still hadn't found an apartment, and the nerves were growing. We started packing up our belongings without knowing where we would end up. We kept having faith that Hashem would guide us and take us to the exact place we had to go.

I was juggling my time between taking care of the children, still trying to find a school for my daughter, and keeping a close eye and tending to Shalva. Through all this my husband was working full-time. The packing was left to me, which was tiring, draining, and exhausting. Every time an apartment seemed like it could possibly be an opportunity for us, I felt so much excitement. I'd call the number, and they would straight out tell me that for our family size, it would be too small.

We continued to daven, asked around, and searched. Finally, in mid-December, there were two rentals that came up. I quickly asked them the price and arranged a meeting time that night. I then contacted my husband with the great news that we have two appointments of rental homes to look at that night, and he should make sure to be home by 7:00 p.m.

I quickly arranged a babysitter and told myself that between one of the two that we were going to see, we would make one of them happen. That day, I packed some more until the children came home. I fed them dinner, did homework, shower time, playtime, and put them to bed on time.

I was showered and ready to go by the time my husband came home from work. He quickly showered and got dressed. He had a quick bite, the babysitter came, and we were off to check out the rental homes.

We went to one of them, and we took our time to look around. But the setup didn't quite suit us. The bedrooms were split into two separate levels of the home. I didn't feel comfortable with that as we have young children. I felt it safest that the bedrooms should all be on one level.

We then went to check out the other rental home. We looked around, and right away, we both looked at each other and said this is perfect. The bedrooms are all together on the same level and the children have space to move and play. On the spot, we told the agent we were interested. The agent was very friendly, chatted with us a bit, and said he'd get back to us soon.

The next morning, the agent reached out to me for my email address to send me a contract to sign. I called my husband with the most wonderful news, and we both felt very grateful. We knew and felt that Hashem was always looking out for us. Not only was the rental home perfectly set up and spacious for our family size, but it was within our budget. In the midst of all our challenges, we felt this was a hug from Hashem.

Now that we finalized a rental it gave me a boost of energy to pack more. So, I packed up and hired movers. My kids were anxiously excited when we told them the news. They couldn't wait to see the new rental apartment that we would be moving into.

A few days before we actually moved in, I hired cleaning help to do a thorough cleaning. I was slowly transferring some items into the new rental home. As the children were so curious to see it already, one day, we decided to take the children with us over to the house. They were so excited and felt so blessed. They couldn't wait for the moving day to arrive. Our kids couldn't stop counting down.

The movers came bright and early on a Friday morning. It took about four hours until they were done loading and unloading everything and putting the furniture and beds in the correct spots in the right rooms where they belonged. While the movers were packing things out of our house, some neighbors came to say goodbye. One neighbor that I became really close with was so sweet. She bought us two yummy, iced coffees and a bunch of donuts. We got a few other platters, cakes, and cookies with nice notes from different neighbors. As much as we were excited to move, we would miss our neighbors. They were such amazing, warm kind-hearted people.

After everything was packed out of our apartment, I double-checked to make sure we didn't leave anything behind. I then started cleaning up. I swept and threw away lots of garbage. I then drove to the new rental home and started unpacking as much as I was able to without being in anyone's way.

After the kids finished school, my husband went to pick them up and went back to the other apartment to finish cleaning it well. He mopped, sprayed down the counters, and bathrooms etc. I stayed at home trying to unpack as much as I could before having to get ready for Shabbos.

The coffee, donuts, and pastries got us by through the day as I was unpacking, and my husband was cleaning. My husband took our kids out for lunch, to pizza. Moving day was a very exciting, memorable day for the kids.

We went away for Shabbos as the house was not set up and ready for us yet. Sunday was a very busy day. My husband spent the day with the children and did some errands while I stayed home unpacking. I started with the bedrooms, so we would be able to sleep at home that night. I started with preparing the beds and putting the clothing away neatly. This way, we can all sleep at home and have access to our clothing. When I was done with the bedrooms, I continued unpacking as much as I could as the time was ticking, and I was racing the clock. I knew that my husband would be working the rest of the week, and it would be difficult for me to unpack while having to manage the home, take care of all the kids, take them to school, and pick them up without any help.

I accomplished a lot though it was a huge job, I had lots more to do. My husband came home, and he bought food for supper. I bathed the kids and put them to bed. They went to sleep so nicely and so excitedly on their new beds and linen in the new rental home. There was so much excitement in the air.

What a long, exhausting day, though I felt very accomplished and productive. I then showered, got ready for bed, said Shema, and fell asleep as soon as I hit the pillow.

The next day was the beginning of my new routine. Since we moved, it has taken time for transportation to set into place. I had to drive all my kids to school and pick them all up each at their own time. I felt like I was a shuttle service. In between dropping off and picking our kids up, I was taking care of Shalva, doing laundry, cleaning the house, and preparing supper. I tried to unpack as well. The unpacking was a long process as I didn't have much time and I was doing it all by myself. This new schedule was a hard adjustment for me to get used to. My goal was to be done unpacking and totally settled in before my due date.

Three weeks prior to my due date, we had a scheduled procedure for Shalva. Two weeks prior to the scheduled procedure appointment, the billing department of the hospital reached out to me to confirm the appointment and said that our insurance was out of network and there was no coverage. The only way to go about this is, if we have insurance that has out of state and out of network coverage that the hospital and doctor take. Otherwise, we would be responsible for paying out of pocket unless we find another doctor in this network.

She said they accept group insurance, or I should speak with my insurance company to see if there's anything they can do. Group insurance wasn't a possibility for us as neither my husband nor I worked for a company that offers health insurance benefits. She gave me her number and direct extension to call her back after I figured out what to do.

I called my insurance agency and told them that the insurance was not covering Shalva's procedure. I asked them what there was to do about that. They said they would do further research into this and get back to me.

If we wanted to keep the procedure appointment, we had to figure this out and take care of it in a quick and timely manner. My insurance agency understood that and took this to heart. They were proactive and on top of our case.

The agency spoke with the insurance company, and they said it shows that this doctor is in the insurance network. She called me back excited to tell me that and offered to make a three-way call to the billing department of the hospital. I accepted and appreciated the offer and that's what we did.

We called the billing department and dialed in her extension. I told them I had the insurance agency on the phone line with me and then had her speak. They spoke for a few minutes, and it seemed that they would take that insurance if it had out of coverage benefits which mine didn't have. We then ended the call.

The agency called me back after the call and said she'd do further research to see what can be done, if there's a way to add out of network to our plan. I thanked her immensely and she said she'd keep me posted.

Throughout the day I spoke with the insurance agency back and forth as they were working really hard to make this happen. Being that they were very proactive and assertive it was very calming and hopeful for me.

For the next couple of days this continued. We went back and forth with phone conversations with the insurance agency. Some three-way calls to the hospital billing department, and some direct calls to the billing department. I also spoke to the doctor's team and was just trying to brainstorm different ways to make this work.

CHAPTER: 28

As days passed and the insurance agency was working endlessly on trying to figure this out for us, I was getting nervous. The hospital didn't want to hold the appointment if I wouldn't be taking it, the pressure was hefty.

The doctor's secretary called and offered to push off the appointment to give me some more time to work on the insurance. I thought about it for a moment and said I was due three weeks after the scheduled procedure. I want this done before I give birth so that if I'm overdue, I don't go into labor during the procedure. I want to be there with her fully, and once the baby is born, I don't know how I'd be able to manage that. With that being said, I thanked them and chose to decline that offer. I said I wanted some more time, if possible, to try to work things out, as I really want it done before the arrival of my new baby.

Later on, I got a call from the billing department. She said they could offer me a discount if I paid out of pocket, and we could arrange a payment plan. I asked her how much it would be, and she said she'd get back to me.

In the meantime, I decided to call the man who got us to go to Boston in the first place. He was so helpful all along, I figured, let me try. I spoke with him and explained the whole situation that I was dealing with. I asked him for advice. He told me to get in contact with an insurance advocate agency, and he gave me the contact number and told me to call right away. He said I should tell them he sent me to them, and this is an urgent situation.

Immediately after hanging up the phone, I called the number he gave me. I told them everything and answered all their questions. I then gave them my email address so they can send me some forms to fill out. They said I should fill it out right away and send it back ASAP without any delay so they can get the process rolling.

I called the insurance agency to update them and let them know that I got an insurance advocate team to help us out as well. Hopefully, between them all, we can work something out. I then printed out the forms, filled them out, signed them, and sent them back.

I also contacted the insurance company to see if there was anything they could do from their end, and then both the agencies continued to speak with each other directly.

Dealing with the doctor, insurance agency, insurance advocate team, and hospital billing team, I was literally on the phone all day for days. And they all were really trying hard to help us and make this happen.

The hospital billing department got back to me with a quote. However, it was totally unaffordable, even if we were to make a payment plan. We have so many medical bills to pay as is. I said I'd discuss it with my husband and get back to her. I spoke it over with my husband, it was not practical and unrealistic. I got back to her and told her that's not an option for us, I can't afford it.

It was Friday, and the procedure date was nearing. It was ten days away, and at that point, the hospital called me and said they understood that we were working on it, however they couldn't hold our slot unless we guaranteed to keep it. I told them I'd call the insurance agency and advocate team to see if there are any updates or good news on their end for us. She said I should get back to her before the end of the day.

I quickly called both the advocate team and agency one at a time and told them the pressure was on. The hospital needs an answer today. They both said, unfortunately there's nothing to do yet but ask if we can have the appointment held until Monday.

I called the hospital back and asked if I could have until Monday, and they agreed. I thanked them so much for their time and patience and for all the back and forth.

Over the weekend, I davened and was thinking and discussing it with my husband. What's going to happen, what will we do if the insurance doesn't come through for us etc. My husband said let's just trust in Hashem. Everything always worked out until now, and we did all the hishtadlus (efforts) we possibly could do. Now all we had to do was let Hashem guide us.

After taking everyone to school and being home with just Shalva, I started the calls. I called the agency, and they said they did everything they possibly could. At this point, there is really nothing they can do. She apologized and felt so bad. I thanked her so much for all her time, energy, patience, and devotion. She asked me to please let her know what ends up happening, and I should be in touch with her if she can help out in any other possible way.

I then called the insurance advocate, and they said the process takes time. On their end, they sped things up, but they have to wait for the insurance company. So right now, we are at a still point waiting. I thanked them for everything!

I then called the hospital to update them. I said I really appreciate her for giving me this extra time, and for all the many back and forth phone conversations we had. I thanked her for her time and patience and updated her. I apologized that it was a long process with constant back-and-forth calls, though unfortunately at this time we couldn't get the out of network coverage. I told her how badly I wanted this done before my baby is born though I'm going to let G-D run the show. She felt bad and told me if it works out with insurance coverage, I should call her back at any time. With that, I thanked her and ended the call.

I felt confused about what was going to be now. In the back of my mind, I was hoping that somehow, miraculously, I'd get a call that the insurance is covered and that the network or the doctor would accept this, though it was not realistic to think that way. I kept reminding myself Hashem had a plan, and maybe it was just not the right timing. I did everything I possibly could, and clearly, Hashem was telling us no. After internalizing that, I felt a lot more content.

We just had to figure out what we would do if there was an emergency situation, we continued to daven. The other team of doctors took our insurance, and they told us they would continue taking care of Shalva, which was also reassuring. We talked about it a little and said maybe we would look into the Children's Hospital of Philadelphia. We heard great things about them over the years. Then we brushed this topic under the rug for the time being.

In the meantime, we had a virtual follow up visit with the Vascular Anomaly team in Boston. Shalva seemed to be doing well and they were happy with her progress. I then discussed the insurance issues with them and told them I was not sure what was going to be. They said we would love to keep your case, however if you can't settle the insurance, they feel confident with us going to CHOP (Children's Hospital of Philadelphia). They said they knew some doctors and surgeons there and gave me recommendations. They said if I decide to switch, I can always still call them for advice, as another opinion, or with questions. That was really sweet and reassuring.

I discussed that with my husband, and he said that's a great idea. If CHOP takes her insurance, it would be an ideal situation. The commute is only about one and a half hours, so traveling is a lot more feasible. The doctors and surgeons are credible, and we can always stay in touch with Boston. My husband was thrilled with this idea. It was a lot more practical in so many ways.

After speaking about it, I called Boston and updated them. They said we should really feel comfortable reaching out to them at any time, they really loved Shalva. I decided I'm not going to schedule anything until after I gave birth and I put all of this to the side.

My mother called me to see if my brother could stay with me for a little bit as his school was right near my house. I said sure. He came to me on Sunday night, and I told him I was due around now, it's perfect that you're staying over. I arranged that if I go into labor in the middle of the night, I will wake him up, so he knows he is babysitting. The timing he came couldn't have been better. Hashem orchestrated it perfectly and beautifully.

With all my other children, I never went into the hospital in the middle of the night. Yet it was such a relief to know if I do I have coverage, and I wouldn't have to worry about who will be there for my kids. One chai Lifeline volunteer girl became very close with us. She became a part of our family. I spoke with her, and she would be on call for me during the day.

Wednesday night I went to bed feeling fine and I told my husband he should get a good night's sleep as he was not going to work the next day. I had a feeling I'd be in the hospital. I had such a strong feeling and I wanted both of us to be well rested.

My husband went to sleep right away, and I couldn't fall asleep. I was just twisting and turning. The last time I checked the clock was 12:30 a.m. and shortly after I finally fell asleep.

At about 1:50 a.m. I woke up with a really heavy contraction. The first thought that came to my mind is that I don't want to go to the hospital as I couldn't handle the thought of having to give birth wearing a mask. When the contraction passed, I closed my eyes to go back to sleep. Eight minutes later I had another contraction, and when this one passed, I decided I was not going to look at the clock anymore. I rolled over, closed my eyes and tried to sleep.

Without timing it, it must've been about every eight minutes that I was having contractions. So, by 2:30 a.m., I decided to call the doctor. I told them my contractions started at 1:50 a.m. I timed the first one but none after that. It must be about that timing in between each contraction, and she told me to come in. My husband woke up hearing me on the phone and asked if everything was okay. I told him I was in labor he jumped out of bed and told me to get ready to go. I called my doula and told her I was getting ready to go.

She said she will leave her house at the same time as me, so I'll keep her posted when I leave.

My husband asked me why I didn't wake him up right away, which he already knew from the past. I have never woken him up in labor unless he heard me on his own. The reason is that I get nervous about giving birth, the pain, and I like being home. So, I go into a bit of a denial stage until the contractions become unbearable. That's also why I don't call the doctor right away. I wait until I know it's happening. I know that my husband takes me seriously, and if I wake him up, he'll want to go in immediately. So, I push it off as long as I can.

I then got up, got dressed, and put on some makeup. My husband looked at me and said, "You're about to give birth, there's no need to beautify yourself." I told him I was almost done. I then woke up my brother and told him I was in labor and going to the hospital.

I texted my doula that we were leaving my house now, and we made our way to the hospital. We got to the hospital about 3:40 a.m. They monitored me and did my vitals and by 4:00 a.m. I was in the delivery room. The doula was there but they didn't let her in to the triage, so she met me in the delivery room. My husband was learning his daf (page of the Talmud) as the doula and midwife assisted me. He was right next to me and was very supportive the whole time. This was the first time I've ever used a doula and midwife, and the experience was unreal.

At 5:30 a.m. the midwife said congratulations on this beautiful, precious, healthy, baby boy! I felt so emotional and took every moment in. I was so grateful to Hashem for a healthy baby. I felt so much joy. This was such a unique experience, giving birth to a healthy baby after everything I've been through with Shalva. I burst into joyful emotional tears and couldn't stop thanking Hashem! I always appreciated health, but this time, I appreciated it so much more. We cannot take anything for granted! I texted my brother to call me as soon as he woke up. I wanted to tell my kids directly as I didn't want them to find out from anyone else.

CHAPTER: 29

As soon as the kids woke up, they checked my room, and we weren't there. They quickly ran and woke up my brother and called me. I told them, "Mazel Tov, you have a brand-new healthy baby brother." They were so excited. They couldn't wait to meet him and see pictures. I told my brother that my husband would be home soon, and they'd see pictures right away.

My husband stayed with me until about 8:15 a.m. Then I sent him home so he could daven, bring the kids to school, and take care of Shalva. As much as I wanted him to be in the hospital with me and the baby, I didn't want the kids to feel any changes. I also wanted their routine and schedule to stay intact as much as possible.

Shalva was so excited to be a big sister and couldn't wait to meet her new baby brother. She went with my husband to buy a car seat and some baby clothing and blankets. She felt like such a big helper and was so proud to be a big sister.

Later in the day, I called my husband as I wanted to fill out the baby's birth certificate. We didn't settle on a name yet, so we discussed it. During my ninth month, I told my husband if we had a boy, there was a name that I love. The meaning to it is really beautiful, and that the holy person that this name is after I love what he stood for. I hope that my baby will live up to his namesake. My husband also really liked the name. Though he had a relative he wanted to name him after. We decided to name the baby both names.

The first Friday night after a boy is born, we have the custom of making a Shalom Zacher. It's a gathering with men to welcome the new baby boy to the world. I spoke to my family and told them I was going to make a small Sholom

Zacher in my house as we recently moved into this neighborhood. My parents and two of my younger brothers came. So did my sister, brother-in-law and their three kids, which really enhanced this momentous occasion. They didn't want to burden me, so they made the food and brought over some yummy fruits and platters for Shabbos.

Friday, my husband had to run to buy some food and drinks to serve for the Sholom Zacher. So, after he came home from Shacharis, he took some kids to school and started doing all the last-minute errands. He tried to get as much done as fast as possible, as he also needed to pick me up as soon as I'd be discharged.

Some neighbors, family, and friends sent over some goodies and platters for the Sholom Zacher. I got home and saw everything that was sent over it was really special.

My husband came to pick me up. As soon as he entered the room, I told him, before anything, "I want you to go outside our room and look at the door." He couldn't believe his eyes when he saw we were in room 613. He felt another hug from Hashem. This uplifted his spirit more than it already was.

It was a beautiful room, with a beautiful view of the water in room 613. Waking up to the sun rising over the water, what could've been better? I had a great stay. Now, we were waiting for our discharge papers as my husband was looking out the window, taking in the beautiful view for the few minutes he was there. As soon as we got our discharge papers, we headed out right away and went straight home. I was so excited to see my kids and have them meet the cutest new addition to the family.

As soon as I walked in the door, Shalva ran to me and just wanted to hold the baby. I washed her hands with soap and water and let her hold him together with me. Her face lit up and glowed, she is a proud big sister.

She asked me to see his booboo. Being that she was born with a lymphatic malformation, which she calls a booboo, she assumes everyone is born with a booboo. I explained to her that Baruch Hashem, our baby is healthy, and he has no booboo. She was so happy that she couldn't stop looking at him and kissing him gently.

My other kids came running into the living room when they heard we were home, and they were all ecstatic and excited. The house was filled with happiness and joy. It was so heartwarming and uplifting to see the joy in everyone's faces. What a beautiful welcoming home.

My mother was over, and she had already cooked and cleaned the house before I got home. The kids were all bathed and ready for Shabbos. I showered and got ready myself. I then came down and cleaned a bit more as some more family came to drop over platters and wish us Mazel Tov!

We had a beautiful meal. After the meal, we cleaned up and set up for the Sholom Zacher. We had lots of food between what my husband bought and what was sent over. Everyone helped, and we were all very relaxed and calm until people started coming. We were really not expecting so many people as our close friends and relatives don't live within walking distance to us.

It was really nice when my husband's nephew walked in. It made my husband's night, and it really meant a lot to him. As the night progressed, some neighbors came slowly but surely, and the house started filling up with lots of neighbors. As some left, more came. It was a full house. It was a beautiful, uplifting, and nice turnout.

At about 11:00 p.m. as everyone wished Mazel Tov and started heading out, I started putting my children to bed. By the time I came back down all the men have left. Everyone told me to sit and relax as they clean up. So, I sat on the couch with my newborn baby.

By 11:45 p.m., all the food was packed away, and the garbage was done. Everyone started heading for bed. I put my baby into the swing, and my husband and I had some time to talk whilst I swept the floors. Everyone told me to leave it until the morning, and they would sweep, though I like my floors clean. And sweeping is an easy task for me.

As I was almost done, we heard a knock on the door. It was another neighbor who had heard that we were making a Sholom Zachur and stopped by just to wish us Mazel Tov! It was really special. This was a neighbor we have never even met, and he made it his business to come by, which was inspiring. It's really meaningful when people come to join in our Simcha (joyous celebration).

I finished up sweeping and tidying up my house, and I took my baby and called it a night. It was a beautiful Shabbos, and it came and went so fast. Over Shabbos, Shalva seemed a bit pale, and we kept a close look at her.

When Shabbos was over, we put the kids to bed. My parents helped clean up, and then they all went back to their homes.

Sunday morning, as my husband came home from Shul and finished learning his daf (page of the Talmud), he looked at Shalva and said she did not look good, and he was concerned. He decided to take her to the emergency room in CHOP. I stayed home with my three-day old baby and the rest of my children as my husband took Shalva.

I was so emotional, and it was really hard for me. I was always there with her in the hospital, and now there was no way that I was able to go. I was glad she had my husband, though I felt extremely emotional and helpless. The least I could do was be by her side and even that I couldn't do.

The day seemed forever, and time was moving very slowly. I just wanted Shalva to be okay and well and home with me. I tried to hold back my tears when I was around my other children as I didn't want to instill any fear in them. This was a new stage in life, and I wasn't ready for it.

Throughout the day, they did imaging, blood work, and vitals. They admitted her for the night and wanted to keep her monitored. I could not sleep the entire night. I was so worried about Shalva and couldn't bear not being with her. It's a mother's natural instinct to want to be there for their child, especially during times like these.

I davened a lot and shed many tears. I felt very connected to Hashem, and I told Hashem since I was not there, I knew He was there holding her tight. When I thought like that, my spirits were boosted.

Sunday night, my sister-in-law called me up to say that she would come sleep over here for the night. I told her it was okay everyone was home and sleeping. She insisted, this way there's another adult in the house for safety. Plus, she would be there in the morning to help with the kids and drive them to school. It was really thoughtful, and I appreciated that.

Monday morning, as soon as I woke up, I called my husband. He updated me that they would be discharged. What a relief! I felt so excited I couldn't wait for Shalva to be back home. In the meantime, they scheduled a follow up appointment where we would meet the new team of doctors that would be on Shalva's case. I gave the consent for Boston to release her medical history to the doctors here at CHOP.

Being that my kids still didn't have bus transportation, between two of my sisters-in-law and a neighbor, they were very kind and offered to bring my kids to school and pick them up. They said they would continue until a week after the baby's Bris (a ceremony that takes place on the eighth day after the birth of a baby boy when he gets circumcised). What a huge help! I was so grateful and felt really relieved.

We prepared some pekalach (party bags with some nosh) to give out by the Vacht Nacht, which is the night before a baby has a bris the baby needs some extra spiritual protection. So, some kids come and recite the prayer of Shema, and as they leave, we give them a pekalah to go home with.

After the Vacht Nacht was over and everyone went home, I fed my kids dinner, bathed them, and put them to bed on time. As they needed to be up early to get ready, and to be on time to go to Shul for davening, as the Bris is immediately after.

That night, I went with my sister-in-law to a few stores to try to find an outfit to wear. She had so much patience and was very helpful. Baruch Hashem, I found something nice, modest, and elegant to wear.

I came right back home and prepared a room for my parents as they were sleeping over for the night. This way, they would make it on time for the bris in the morning without having to wake up so early to commute. I was planning to wait for them, though they were running late. I was exhausted and called them to say that I'd be going to bed, and they were happy. They wanted me to rest up as much as possible.

The next morning, we all woke up bright and early, showered, got dressed and put our seat belts on in the car as we drove off to Shul. We were stuck in traffic, so it took us some extra time to get there.

It was so meaningful that my parents and all my siblings made an effort to come and some of my husband's family. Some of our neighbors from our six months rental home came, and some friends showed up, and so did the Rabbi from our son's school. It meant so much to us! A Simcha (a celebration of a happy occasion) is only a Simcha when spent with family and friends, and we felt true Simcha (happiness). Each and every person that came really enhanced and made it a beautiful ceremony.

After the bris was over, we took the kids to school and then came straight home. My mother stayed for the next few days to help me with the baby as he recovered from his Bris.

In the meantime, we started homeschooling for my older daughter. She loved the teachers and gained so much. It was so good for her to have a daily routine, schedule, structure, and responsibility. It was great for her in so many ways. The only thing it was missing was friends. She has friends in the neighborhood, so after school hours, she has social time to spend with friends. Throughout all this time, she continued with her violin lessons, and that really kept her going. It was great for her confidence, and she felt so good about herself.

It was great that we started homeschooling, and we would continue it until the end of the year. It was a great temporary solution, though we still needed to find her a school for next year, as this was not a good long-term solution.

I've been in touch with the most incredible Rabbi who's been helping, advocating and trying so hard on my daughter's behalf all year. Between phone calls and text messages back and forth, he dealt with us for hours on end. To this day, he's been helping us tremendously. I don't know if he made my daughter's case his priority, though it definitely seemed that she was his number one priority. I feel forever grateful for all his time, effort, energy, and work on our behalf.

As time moved on and the year was nearing an end, I started getting nervous that we still didn't have a school for the following year. I felt so burnt out from trying and trying, with one rejection after the next, though there was no giving up. I just kept on davening, as a mother's dream is to want the best for their child. I wanted her to be happy and have a normal healthy upbringing. I wanted her to have the opportunity to learn, grow, and blossom.

My heart has been torn and shattered, and I keep on reminding myself that Hashem has a master plan. For whatever reason, she had to go through all this, and so did we. I had people ask me "aren't you turned off that no school accepted her?" When I was asked how this whole situation didn't turn me off, I answered I know this is a nisayon (challenge/test) that we are being faced with. For whatever reason, she needed to go through this in order for her to fulfill her tikun (mission) in life.

Is there pain? Yes, 100%, though at the end of the day I know Hashem is orchestrating all of this. I have no clue why and we may be able to understand later on, or we may not. I know Hashem is perfect, and I'm not. Nothing happens coincidentally and it's all a part of the Master plan!

CHAPTER: 30

As time passed and summer was nearing, the Rabbi called me up and gave me a number to call to set up an interview. I did that right away. I took the first available appointment, and Baruch Hashem, it went well. They pretty much accepted her on the spot. They had hearts and I'm so grateful to them for giving my daughter an opportunity to rise and shine.

She was nervous and excited, which were totally acceptable and normal healthy emotions. We discussed it a lot. During the first half of the summer, she continued with being homeschooled. In the second half of the summer, she went to day camp. The excitement and smile that she had as she got onto the bus on the first day of day camp was worth more than any value of money. She came home from camp glowing from ear to ear. Her face was glowing as she told me about the wonderful day she had. I was so happy she felt like a child. She was able to be with friends and have fun and there was nothing like this. She had the most amazing summer in her life.

Shalva saw all the children going to school, and in the summer, off to camp. She really wanted to be just like everyone else. She wanted to feel big and go to school. I was not ready to send her off, though she kept on asking for it. I told her that big kids that go to school are toilet trained, so we're not ready yet. She was so determined that right then and there she started the process. Within a week, she was fully toilet trained. After I saw her determination and motivation that she really did her part, I had no choice but to do mine and find her a school.

I got a great recommendation for a playgroup of kids her age. I called them up, and they said they had to check if there was room. I told them how determined Shalva was to go to school and how highly recommended this school was. She said she'd get back to me.

I waited patiently for a call. A couple of days past and we got great news. Baruch Hashem, they had a slot available for Shalva. I was so excited I had to tell Shalva right away. As soon as I hung up the phone, I ran to Shalva, I said "Shalva! Guess what?" She said, "what? Tell me! Tell me!" "I have great news for you!" She said, "YAY, I'm going to school after the summer." Yes, I told her Baruch Hashem. We got into school, she was ecstatic, she couldn't wait, she was glowing!

As the summer progressed, day after day, she kept asking when school was starting. She was telling everyone that she was a big girl, and she was going to school. As school was nearing, I bought her a whole new wardrobe of clothing, and my mother bought her a Knapsack and lunchbox with her name on it. She counted down the days with such excitement. The night before school began, I let Shalva choose which outfit she wanted to wear, and we put it aside for the morning. She went to bed so nicely with much excitement for the next day!

In the morning, she jumped out of bed, yay, I'm going to school today. I'm such a big girl! She ate breakfast and got dressed as fast as she was able to and was eagerly awaiting to go to school.

She went to school with a huge smile on her face, gave me a hug and a kiss and waved goodbye. She was so excited and felt so big and proud! It was a really beautiful milestone, and I was very emotional. I couldn't believe my eyes, my princess that the doctors had no hope on life for is starting school. Words cannot express that moment! I had a hard time leaving her, though it helped to see her off to school to a great start with so much joy and happiness.

Baruch Hashem, we were up to a great start to the year. She was doing well, but in the following days, she had a harder time parting from me, which was normal. The whole morning, she was so excited to get ready for school. The whole car ride there, she would speak about school, her teachers, and friends.

When we got there, she was sad that I couldn't stay. I spoke to her and reassured her that I'd pick her up as soon as school was over. I gave her lots of hugs and kisses. When I left, she started crying, which broke my heart. I was not ready to send her, but she was very persistent about going. Her teacher would call me a few minutes later to tell me she calmed down and seemed happy.

This went on for some time. Every day when I came to pick her up, she looked so happy and was excited to tell me everything she learned and did in school. All the projects she made, the toys she played with, and about the friends she had.

Some time passed, and it was a Friday at the beginning of November. She came home from school happy and playful. Later on that day, I bathed her, and she was excited to get dressed and ready for Shabbos. Shortly after the meal, I put her and all my other kids to bed.

Shabbos morning, she woke up and came straight to my room and said, "Mommy, my booboo hurts." She came on my bed and showed it to me. It looked swollen and red with a little lump. I put my finger on it gently to see if it was hard or soft and the temperature of how it felt. The second I touched it, she shouted "ouch!" I knew that was not a good sign as I touched it gently without putting any pressure on it whatsoever.

I ran downstairs as my husband was in the middle of learning his daf (page of the Talmud) before he would go to Shul. I told him to come upstairs. At first, he said he wanted a few minutes so he could finish what he was doing so he wouldn't be late to shul. I told him I think we may have an emergency. He quickly closed his Gemara (Talmud) and ran upstairs with me.

I didn't want Shalva to feel scared, so I told her Daddy came to look at her booboo. She showed it to him, and he tried to touch it, and she again gave a shout ouch, ouch! Being that it was very swollen and red and felt hot and hard, we decided to call Hatzalah (a volunteer emergency medical service).

Hatzalah was here within three minutes. They checked her, and we told them a little about her history. They said she has to be seen and they would take her to the hospital. I really wanted to come, though I couldn't leave my baby behind as he was a full-time nursing baby. The Hatzalah members weren't sure if the Emergency Room and hospital would let the baby come in with us, so they said it was best if my husband goes with her.

The Hatzalah members told us to pack whatever my husband needs for Shalva and himself for the day. Even though it was Shabbos I should keep my phone handy and answer if my husband or hospital calls.

I walked them into the ambulance truck, and kissed Shalva. I told her I wish I could be there with you. Daddy is going to take great care of you, and I'll be davening at home.

As they left, I ran into my house with all my children as tears didn't stop rumbling down my cheeks. I was super emotional, felt helpless, and couldn't just call to check up. I utilized the moments to daven and say Tehillim throughout the day.

My children were nervous as I tried to reassure them that all we could do was daven, which is so powerful, and hopefully the doctors would be the right shaliach (messenger). We ate the meal and tried to stay positive about the situation. My kids were asking me loads of questions, and I told them we won't have updates unless Daddy or the hospital called me. I listened to all of them express their feelings about how nervous they are. They feel so bad for Shalva, and they just wanted Shalva to be totally better and have no more booboos.

It was a very emotionally draining day between keeping my kids calm and taking care of the baby and all the unanswered questions we all had. I recited the entire Tehillim over Shabbos. My kids davened as well, and then they went to play with some neighbors, which was a great healthy distraction for them. Later on in the day, I fed the kids and put them to bed.

I love Shabbos and enjoy every minute of it usually. This Shabbos was exceptionally hard to enjoy, not knowing what was going on with my precious princess. I somehow managed throughout the day, though the last ten minutes felt everlasting.

As soon as Shabbos was over, I spoke to my husband. He said Shalva hadn't eaten since 12:00 p.m. as they wanted her to go in for an MRI. They did bloodwork and some imaging. And now, they're still waiting for an MRI. Being that she couldn't eat, my husband hadn't eaten either, as he couldn't eat in front of her. While she napped, he was able to daven and finish his daf (page of the Talmud). At this point, he was waiting for Shalva to have an MRI and to be admitted into a room. He said he'd let me know as soon there are more updates.

A short while later, my husband called me back and said that they had just been admitted to a room. They said Shalva could eat as there were no available slots for an MRI until the morning. I was happy she was able to eat now, though I felt that it was negligent on the hospital's end to have a three-year-old girl fast for nine hours for no reason. My husband said they told him she could eat until midnight, and then she'd have to fast again. I told him if I was there, I would speak up. Since I'm not, I need him to tell them that we have no problem with her fasting, so long as she has an MRI timing scheduled. So, he spoke to them.

Being that in Boston there was no Bikur Cholim room, now that we were in a different hospital, my husband found out that there was a Bikur Cholim room here. It was a really special treat, and my husband was excited to have access to kosher food.

He then went to the Bikur Cholim room and was amazed at the site. After he finished feeding Shalva and was done eating, he called me up with much amusement. He said he couldn't believe his eyes. The Bikur Cholim room was fully stocked up with everything you can possibly think of, from cutlery to food, drink, coffees, snacks, fruits, vegetables, a bookshelf filled with lots of different Jewish books and Sefarim (Biblical books) Jewish magazines. And Tefillin (Phylacteries). The room was fully stocked and equipped to make the stay at the hospital as homey as it could possibly be. He felt the unity of the Jewish nation. How people really care and think of others. He kept saying Mi K'amcha Yisrael (who's like the nation of Israel). He felt such pride being a part of this beautiful special nation! When we do good deeds, it's an act of a Kiddush Hashem (sanctifying G-D). Being in the hospital is not the place anyone wants to be, though the site of the Bikur Cholim room gave my husband a boost of chizuk (strength).

As he was expressing all this to me, he felt shrivels down his spine and knew Hashem was really watching over and taking care of them. He felt this was another hug from Hashem, which he needed at that time. I was so happy he experienced this as it was incredible.

I asked him to find out if I could come to the hospital with my baby to be with Shalva at her bedside. I was not coping well, knowing that I was so far away from her, and she was going through so much. All I wanted was to be a nurturing Mommy and be by her side, davening, supporting, and advocating for her!

A few minutes later he called me with great news that I can come with my nursing baby. I wanted to come right then and there. My husband suggested since Shalva is sleeping anyways, I should get a good night of sleep. We don't know how long Shalva will be in the hospital. I still really wanted to come, though I knew she was in good hands, so I said I'd come in the morning.

In the meantime, I spoke with my mother and told her about Shabbos and what had been going on with Shalva. I told her I wanted to go to Shalva. Right away she said she'd come over for the night and be with my kids the next day, and so my mother came with my sister. It was a massive help and real support.

In the morning, my boys got dressed and ready for school. They ate breakfast, and I drove them to school as usual. On the way, I spoke to my boys, and I told them that Bubby (Grandma) came, and she's going to stay over and take care of all of them until Daddy gets back home. They were excited that she was over and would get to spend time with her as that's always so much fun, though they were sad that I was leaving. I reassured them that I was just a phone call away and we would speak every single day. I explained that Shalva needed her mommy to be there with her, which they understood.

I then came back home and packed my bags to get ready to go. My mother and sister wanted to treat me out for breakfast before my journey, though I just wanted to be by Shalva already. I thanked them for the offer and declined. They understood and took my daughter out with them. It was so good for her to have that attention, especially during this time when she was nervous about Shalva.

I've never driven cross-state myself, so I was nervous. I told myself to be brave and said I'll do anything for Shalva. The entire ride, I was just talking to Hashem, asking Him to help me get there safely. I said some Tehillim that I knew by heart. Before I knew it, I arrived at the hospital. That was the first and last time I drove myself across states. Looking back, I'm really proud that I pushed myself to have the courage to drive. I honestly felt Hashem guided me the entire ride as I was never able to brave myself up again to drive cross- state on big highways and bridges. Though when it came to Shalva, I'd do anything and everything for her! Nothing will stop me or get in the way.

I parked in the parking lot, took my baby and the suitcase I packed, and quickly went into the hospital. I went straight up to Shalva's room. As soon as she heard my voice, she turned her face towards me with a beautiful glowing smile. It was such a comforting moment for both of us! I washed my hands with soap and water, ran to Shalva, and gave her a big, huge hug and kiss. She wanted me to snuggle with her. My baby fell asleep during the car ride and was still asleep, so I was able to.

I thanked my husband for all his help and told him he should go home to be with the kids and get a well-rested, good night's sleep. He said he'd first go get some food from the Bikur Cholim room for Shalva and me as he wanted to make sure we would eat.

He got us some food and drinks and we spoke for a few minutes. Then he kissed Shalva goodbye, gave her a bracha, and told her he'd be back another day. I thanked him for being such a good, devoted father and for all his help and told him to let me know when he got back home.

Being that it was Sunday, Shalva went in for an MRI. So, we had to wait for the results to come in. Other than that, not much went on. They just took her vitals throughout the day and kept her monitored. I gave her lots of attention and spent lots of quality time with her. She was happy the baby came along as she was able to play with him, and that made her less homesick. He gave her lots of entertainment and fun.

Every night I'd snuggle with Shalva and my baby, say Shema and some Tehllim with her until she would fall into a deep sleep. When my baby was in a deep enough sleep, I was be able to transfer him to his carriage and then call it a night, until he'd wake up for a nursing.

Her teacher called to see why Shalva was absent. I told her everything that happened from Shabbos morning up until this point. Her teacher listened so empathetically and was the most incredible woman. She took Shalva to heart, she gave me lots of resources, sent over school projects, arts and crafts, and presents to occupy Shalva with. Shalva really felt her love and compassion.

She called every single day with the entire class, and they all sang Shalva a Refuah Shelaima (get well) song. That was Shalva's highlight of the day. She would wait for the call. As her friends and teacher would talk and sing her face lit up and glowed. The times we missed the call, they would leave a voicemail and Shalva would listen to it repeatedly many times. These calls made such an impact on her.

Besides the teacher calling with the class every day, she would call every night to see how Shalva was feeling and doing. How was I managing, and how my kids at home were doing? She offered to help with my other children at home, and she meant it sincerely and lovingly. She felt so bad about what the family was going through. I took her up on the offer for Friday afternoon. She arranged a ride for my kids to go to her straight from school until they would be picked up without any pressure of time. She's so special and went way above and beyond.

My son mentioned it was his birthday, and she made him a small ice cream party in her house. He felt like a million dollars. He remembers that day and talks about it all the time. It's a birthday that he'll never forget.

CHAPTER: 31

Monday morning came, and I met the team of doctors who were on Shalva's case. They checked on her and asked me lots of questions, and I told them everything. They said they wanted to put her on Augmentin in the meantime. I told them in the past when she had a swollen infection, they gave her Keflex. However, they said they want to stick with Augmentin.

It seemed that the medication she was on all these months was not helping her out. They said they would temporarily take her off of it while she was on antibiotics and see how she did. After a few days of her being monitored, they didn't see improvement. They decided they wanted to do a culture, which means they would put her under anesthesia and open her up a bit to get some tissue out and test the tissue for an infection.

I kept on telling them that based on the history, it seemed like her lymphatic malformation was acting out, though they were very convinced it was just an infection. I didn't think so and kept on telling them it was the LM (Lymphatic Malformation). They insisted it wasn't.

Later on that day, the anesthesiologist team came to speak to me about the anesthesia for the culture. I asked them if the culture comes out negative once she's under anesthesia can they do a procedure for her LM. They said that's not their department and they would have their team speak to the other doctors. I said before I sign any consent form, I want to know. They understood and said they would let me know later on.

At about 8:30 p.m., our night nurse came in and told us that Shalva couldn't eat or drink after midnight due to the culture procedure in the morning. I asked her if she heard back from the doctors. She said she didn't even know there was a concern, and I explained to her what I wanted. I then told her so long as we were all on the same page and there was a timing for the procedure. She heard me out and said she'd relay my messages.

At around midnight, she came back to me and said she sent a message over to the doctor and was waiting for a response. In the meantime, Shalva is sleeping, so I'd let her fast until the morning. After the nurse left me, I decided to email one of the teams from Boston Hospital, telling them what's been happening. I asked them what they suggested and for their advice. I sent along some images, so they get an idea of what it looks like now. At around 5:30

a.m. I decided to email another team of doctors from Boston Hospital as well.

At about 7:30 a.m., the nurse practitioner from the team of doctors I emailed the night before called me up and said she reviewed the email and images and discussed it with the doctor. They felt my suggestion was a very good idea. They said that based on the images, what she told them and the past history they had with her, it seems like she needs some sort of intervention as it seems that her lymphatic malformation is acting out. She said I could have the hospital call her. I thanked her so much and told her I'd be in touch with her.

As soon as I hung up with her, my phone rang, and it was the nurse practitioner from the other team of doctors. She said the same. I asked her if she'd be willing to speak to the doctors I'm dealing with here, and she said of course.

A few minutes later, the doctors and anesthesiologists all came into the room together and asked me to sign the consent. I asked them if they had spoken to the doctor about what I discussed. They said they spoke to the head doctor of the department, and she said it seemed like it was an infection and at this time, they would not do any other procedure.

I asked them why she was on antibiotics, and they said to treat an infection, so I said it doesn't seem to be working. They said they'd perhaps switch antibiotics to something a bit stronger. I then asked what's the point of the procedure, and they said to pinpoint exactly what infection it was to know which antibiotics to treat her with. So, I asked why she was taking anything now, and they said so it doesn't get any worse.

I then told them that I had reached out to Boston, and they agreed with me. I said they would be more than happy to speak with your team. I gave them their number, and they said they would give it over to the head director doctor of the team. I told them that one of the Boston NPs called me back to see what was going on. I told them what they had just said and handed the resident my phone.

After their conversation, they said at this point, it was getting late, and since I hadn't signed yet and no decision had been made, Shalva could eat until we came up with some sort of solution or agreement. Shalva was so happy to eat as she was starving. I fed her right away while everything got resolved.

A short while after, I got another call from Boston. They told me they spoke with the doctor here, and they were convinced it was an infection. If we were in Boston, they would do an intervention. Being that I'm not, I should just do the culture test for now, and we will take it from there. I was not happy about that, though I knew at this point I had no choice. So later that day, the anesthesiologist team came to me again to sign consent forms, I was not happy about it, though I signed.

That night they switched her antibiotics, took her off of the Augmentin, and started giving her Clindamycin. I asked if they could give her some probiotics along with it, and they said that being she was on the immune suppressant medication, she shouldn't have probiotics for at least thirty days from when she stopped her last dose of that medication.

That didn't sound right to me, so I reached out to my father's friend, whom I spoke to every while, the Infectious disease doctor. I updated him with everything and then asked him about the probiotics. He said he would do further research and get back to me.

Shalva fasted Thursday night, and the culture was scheduled for Friday morning. My heart was broken as I was not comfortable with this. I didn't feel it was necessary. I felt they were putting her under the knife and opening her up for no reason. It was hurtful to me that they wouldn't hear me out, but it wasn't in my control.

My husband packed up stuff for me, Shalva, the baby, and himself. He picked up some things from Shalva's teacher and headed to the hospital after my kids went to school. When my daughter came home, someone was there to babysit. Knowing it was my son's birthday, my daughter surprised him and baked him a beautifully decorated birthday cake. My mother cooked and made Shabbos and brought everything over to our house as my parents were staying with my children in our house over Shabbos.

On the way to our house, they picked my children up from Shalva's teacher's house. They came home to a beautifully set up surprise birthday party that my daughter worked really hard on. My daughter told me earlier just because we were in the hospital, she wanted her brother to feel good and special on his birthday. There's no reason that his birthday should be forgotten and uncelebrated. It was so beautiful and special to see how caring and loving my daughter is. Until this very day, my son says this was his favorite birthday. He felt so much love and care. Since I couldn't physically be there, I called him to wish him a happy birthday. I sang to him and ordered him a few birthday presents from Amazon. He felt so special. It was the least I could do.

Back at the hospital, what happened was Shalva woke up bright and early. I was hoping she would sleep in late, but that didn't happen. I kept her busy and entertained. When she asked to eat, I explained to her that the doctors were going to put her to sleep, and I could feed her when she woke up.

They finally called us downstairs to the triage room before she entered the OR. While we waited, she kept listening to the voicemail from her class over and over again. I read her some books and played with her, and she also got to play with her baby brother. It was so cute how she tried explaining to him what she was experiencing and going through while we waited for the doctors to come and put her to sleep.

When the anesthesiologist came in the room, I again told them I was nervous about this and didn't feel comfortable putting her under the knife. Though it is what it is. The surgeons came in, and I again told them that if they see no signs of infection during the culture and imaging while Shalva is asleep, I really want her to have a procedure as I feel that's what she needs, and then I signed the consent form.

The anesthesiologists were ready to take her to the OR. Since I had my baby with me, they didn't let me walk her, and she was not parting from me. I asked them if they could put her to sleep on the bed in this room with me and they agreed. I snuggled my head next to her and held her hands as they put her to sleep while I said some Tehillim.

I then waited in the room with my baby and nursed him to sleep as I said more Tehillim, while I waited for Shalva to come out of the OR. I was not at ease and couldn't wait for Shalva to come out. This did not sit well with me.

Finally, after waiting some time, the culture procedure was over. They came to the room to tell me how it went. They said that based on the imaging and from the naked eye, there were no signs of infection. The tissue will be sent to the lab, and the result can take anywhere between twenty-four to seventy-two hours to get back. She said the doctor is going to come to speak with me soon and I can ask all my questions. And she said, in a few minutes, Shalva will be brought to me.

A couple minutes passed. A nurse came with Shalva, and together, she guided us towards the elevators to take us to Shalva's room. As the doors of the elevators opened, I saw the doctor. She said she just went to our room looking for us to take a look at Shalva and speak with me.

She stayed in the elevators as we went in, and we all headed to Shalva's room together. The nurse gently transferred Shalva to her bed, and I thanked her for all her help, and she left the room.

The doctor spoke to me and said they were happy Shalva seemed to do well. They would have to wait for the lab results to come back, which can take one to three days. She then said they would keep her on the Clindamycin in the meantime.

I had a lengthy talk with the doctor about how I felt. If we're continuing these antibiotics anyway, how come we needed the culture? She reiterated that the culture would determine the exact infection. Then we discussed the immune suppressant medication she was taking up until this hospital stay, and they felt that perhaps she should restart with it after she's done the antibiotics that she's on. I was hesitant. I told them she's been very moody with the medication, and it's supposed to help shrink the cells, and we are here now because her lymphatic malformation swelled up and inflamed.

They said there's another medication, though it'll only work if Shalva has that exact genetic mutation, and they will test her tissue to find out. The results will take a couple of months. In the meantime, she thought it would be a good idea to continue back to the medication she's been taking.

I told them it's such a strong medication and being that I saw firsthand how it didn't help, I'm not willing to give her such strong medication. I said I tried it out all this time, and I want her to get better, but if it's not doing its job, there's no reason to give it. She heard me out and said it was my choice. She said I should think about it some more and maybe I'll change my mind. She said she'll touch base with me by Monday, and by that time, we should have the results back from the culture they took.

Shortly after, my husband arrived. I updated him with everything that went on. He saw I didn't look happy as I felt I was forced into putting my daughter into an unnecessary procedure. He understood my pain and stood by my side.

Over Shabbos, we had a lot of time to think things through and discuss everything. We both felt the same way in terms of the medication for Shalva. In the meantime, Shalva was just being monitored. They were doing her vitals around the clock, daily blood work, and they didn't have the results back from the lab yet. It was nice having my husband spend Shabbos with us in the hospital. It was a certain feeling of security, and his presence brought in a beautiful Shabbos feeling with having Kiddush and singing Shabbos Zemiros (songs) by the meals. With his learning, we felt the spirit of Shabbos, which was uplifting. It was also helpful as we were able to take turns giving Shalva and the baby full attention.

CHAPTER: 32

As soon as Shabbos was over, I called my mother to see how the kids were doing. I then spoke to my children, and they told me all about Shabbos. I told them my husband would be coming home tonight, though by the time he gets home it'll be late. They'd be asleep, and they would see him first thing in the morning. They were excited to see him. And of course, they asked when I was coming home with Shalva and the baby. I said I still didn't know.

My husband packed up and said goodbye to us. Shalva got so emotional as she just wanted to go back home. We told her as soon as she's able to, Daddy will be back here to pick us up. He hugged and kissed her, and she got so emotional she didn't want him to leave. He stayed a few more minutes to give her some more attention, and then he had to go as it was getting late. He was tired, and he still had to drive home.

Sunday, the nurses and doctors came in to check on Shalva. They said as of now, the culture looks negative, though they will wait another day to see if it becomes positive. In the meantime, it was just the weekend staff. There was not much going on and no updates. We would have to wait until tomorrow.

I took walks with Shalva and my baby around the unit. We went to the Bikur Cholim room to get some food and snacks and walked around the hospital a little to get a change of scenery. I played with some toys with her, read her some books, did some coloring and arts and crafts, and made a beaded bracelet. I tried to give her a good day in the hospital.

After I fed her supper, I gave her a shower, then I said Shema with her, and put her to sleep after a long, fun-filled day for her. She was tired and fell asleep relatively quickly.

Monday morning, we woke up from the nurses coming in to check on Shalva's vitals. I then fed her breakfast and spoke to my other children. I wished them a great day in school and told them I missed them. They wanted to know what was going on with Shalva and when she would be discharged. I told them I didn't know anything yet; I'm waiting for the doctors to come around to get some updates. Hopefully, by the time they come home from school, I'll have some more information to give them.

A few hours passed, and the doctor made their rounds. They told me the culture came back negative. Since it came back negative, they want her to continue with the Clindamycin for a total of three weeks from her first dosage. And they would do some more imaging and blood work today.

I was very grateful there was no infection, and I thanked Hashem for that. At the same time, I felt terribly shattered. I had lots of resentment towards the fact I had no say. I knew all along it wasn't an infection, and my cute little precious princess had to go under the knife for absolutely no reason. It was very upsetting to me.

Shortly after, the main doctor came into the room, and she said I'm sure you heard the lab results came back, and the culture came back negative. I answered yes, I heard, and that's no surprise to me as I knew all along it was her lymphatic malformation acting out, not an infection. I'm not sure if it's ego or what it is though the doctors were not able to admit that. They still held strongly that it was an infection. They said it probably came back negative because of the antibiotics she was on. With that being said I asked whether it was a little negligent to put my child under anesthesia under the knife with all the risks and side effects, knowing that she was on antibiotics and that they might not get accurate results. They refused to apologize for this terrible error. They said it was great, and that meant the antibiotics were working. I said I didn't need her to get cultured to find out that the antibiotics she was on were working.

I felt lots of frustration. The doctors just had to be right, so they were defending what they did. The more they were trying to give me answers, the more I questioned their actions. I felt very hurt, my child had to suffer on Friday for absolutely no reason.

I then went on and asked what the plans were for moving forward. She said maybe we should restart the other medication, and she asked me if I thought it over. I said I had a lot of time to think it through and I discussed it with my husband. Being that it's supposed to shrink it, it's pretty clear that it didn't work. I don't want her back on it. She tried talking me into it and after a while, she realized I had made my decision, and I wasn't backing down on it.

She then went on to say there is no cure! The scientists are still trying to do more research on more medications, though so far, they're using the medication we already tried and another that works only if the patient has a specific, exact cell mutation. All this is to treat the symptoms. I told them it seemed like it was just a band aid and that we're not getting a cure and we're not getting to the core of the issue. She said exactly and repeated there is no cure, and the scientists are trying to do more research on the symptoms.

At that moment, a thought popped into my head, which changed my life forever. I realized I was talking to doctors. They are human beings. Humans make mistakes in life. With human beings, there are lots of trials and errors, and there is a limit to how knowledgeable a person can be. I said Hashem is the master and creator of the world. He was the one that gave Shalva life and had her be born with a lymphatic malformation. It was all for a purpose! Hashem is perfect just like He made her this way, He has the cure. The only way Shalva can be cured is if Hashem wants her to be, and that's where Tefillos have such power on our end. On the doctor's end, there is no cure. They are just treating symptoms. It was a beautiful, uplifting moment that changed the way I viewed my life and everything that I had to deal with.

As upset as I felt that the way she was treated was negligent, this thought was very comforting and healing. Had I not gone through this with Shalva I would never have had such an awakening that transformed my life.

From all the times I've been in the hospital with Shalva, ever since she came home from the hospital the first time, this was the most traumatic hospital experience. Yet at the same time, it was the biggest gift and a real eye opener. Looking back to this time in the hospital I always have such mixed emotions. From the trauma I experienced to the gift and blessing to really feel, see, and know that Hashem is the Master of the world and is the Ultimate Healer. Knowing and believing that is really healing in itself. I thank Hashem for this trauma, as the result of it was the biggest gift.

The doctors were all top notch and very professionally educated. They did their job well, and I have lots of gratitude for all that they did despite the fact I felt that Shalva had been mistreated. There was still lots of warmth, sensitivity, patience, and professionalism. I understood that doctors know as much as they were educated in, and any further research they did, as well as experience from trial and error. I accept that the doctors don't have all the answers. With all their knowledge and resources, they try and do their best. My job is to recognize that Hashem is the ultimate Healer and Guide to the doctors, and that everything that happened was orchestrated perfectly by Hashem. My job is to rely solely on Hashem and daven that the doctors are the perfect shaliach (messenger).

Later in the day, they told me the great news now that the lab work came back. The imaging and blood work have been stable, and Shalva looks and is acting well, eating well with a hearty appetite, active, and playful. She will be able to go home tomorrow.

I was really excited. I quickly called my husband to share the great news that tomorrow Shalva will be discharged. I told him after he feeds the kids breakfast, gets the kids ready, and sends our children off to school in the morning, he should daven and then come straight to the hospital. He said he would wake up early to learn, and if he doesn't finish his daf (page of the Talmud), he will bring his Gemara (Talmud) to the hospital and continue to learn as he waits for us to be discharged. I told him I'd try to find a babysitter to be there for our children in case we were not home by the time they got home from school.

As soon as I hung up, I made a few phone calls. I arranged for a babysitter, I told her since I couldn't pick her up, I would pay for a car service to drive her over to my house, and when I got home, I could take her back.

That night, when I put Shalva to bed, I told her I had great news for her. I said now I'm going to say Shema with you, and then you will go straight to sleep. In the morning, when you wake up, the nurses will do your vitals as usual. We will eat breakfast, and Daddy is going to be coming right away. Her face lit up as she threw her arms in the air. Yay! Yay! I then went on to tell her Daddy was coming, not to stay and she looked worried. I then said Daddy was coming to pick us up and take us home! She started jumping up and down with such excitement in bed!

She told me she wanted to go to sleep fast so it could be the morning already. I told her that's a great idea. I then closed the lights and the curtains, snuggled her into bed, said Shema, and she fell asleep excitedly and peacefully.

She woke up bright and early and started saying, "Yay, Daddy's coming soon!" Then she asked me to call him. I called him up and let her speak to him. With such excitement in her voice, she asked, "Daddy, when will you be here already?" He said after the kids go to school, he said he's going to daven and come right on over.

I dressed her and my baby. The nurse then came in to take her vitals and confirm that today we were being discharged and the doctors would be around before hand.

I then went with Shalva and my baby to the Bikur Cholim room to get them food to eat for breakfast and made myself a coffee. We then came back into Shalva's room to eat. After breakfast was over, we cleaned up the food, and I started cleaning up the room and packing up all our belongings.

Then I nursed my baby, he took a nap, and Shalva got to play with some toys. While she was playing, she told me, "One minute, I want to look out the window to see if I see Daddy." She said, "I see lots of cars. I don't see Daddy." Then she's looked and looked and said, "I see a man. Maybe that's Daddy." Then she said, "oh no, he crossed the street." After a few minutes, I asked her if I should read her a book while she waited for Daddy to come. She liked that idea, so she sat on my lap as I read her a story. I then played with her, and shortly after, she heard someone by the door. She looked, and her face lit up with a huge smile. She started clapping yay, Daddy's here!

A little while later, the doctors came in to check up on Shalva. They spoke to me at length and told me about the medication that she was previously on.

She said in the past they had other parents who thought the medication wasn't helping, and within a month, they came begging for the medication back. They said we could hold off, and at any given time. If I change my mind or feel that Shalva needs it, I should let them know, and they'd be more than happy to prescribe it to her.

They gave me instructions regarding going home and said we would have a virtual follow up in ten days from now. In the meantime, they will schedule an appointment for us to come down and see the whole team of doctors in the clinic in about four to six weeks.

I have lots of Hakaros Hatov (gratitude) to all the doctors and surgeons, and I apologized for speaking to them with such frustration. They validated my feelings and understood that as a mother, I just want the best for my child.

If I didn't feel that the treatment was proper, it's understandable why I felt frustrated. I asked for forgiveness and thanked them.

A few minutes later, the nurse came in with the discharge papers and went through them with us. She gave us a magnet to hang on our fridge with the hospital numbers and contact information. We thanked her and started heading out.

As we left the room, Shalva's face was shining bright. She was so excited she started singing and chanting her own little song, "bye bye booboo, bye bye hospital Baruch Hashem I'm all better, and I'm going home!" In the parking lot, she couldn't wait to get in the car. She felt so excited to be out of the hospital, and she thanked Hashem that she was able to go home.

We made a rest stop on the way home and continued driving. She was really hungry, so we decided before we got home to treat her to supper. We gave her options of what she was in the mood of, and based on that, we made a decision on where to go.

After we ate, we took her to Rita's and let her choose any ice cream she wanted. She's been through such a rough and tough time that I just wanted her to feel good. After she was done, we came straight home.

My kids came running to the door with such excitement to greet us, especially Shalva. They made lots of welcome home and Refuah Shelaima signs and hung them on the front door, all around the walls of the house, her bedroom door, and inside her bedroom. She got such a beautiful, warm, and loving welcome.

My husband then stayed home with everyone as I drove the babysitter home. I thanked the babysitter so much I told her that even though I paid her, it was such a chessed, and I really appreciated her help.

That night, bedtime did not exist in our house. There was way too much excitement, joy and happiness. There were lots of questions and discussions with all the kids amongst themselves, with Shalva, and with us.

As it got late, the kids made their way to shower and put on pajamas, and I put them all to bed. They were so happy to have me put them to bed that they asked that we don't go back to the hospital! I told them, let's just continue davening and hopefully, no more emergencies. They all went to sleep feeling happy and content, knowing we were all united back at home together.

The regular daily routine and schedule continued for everyone, Baruch Hashem. During this stay in the hospital, the kids finally got school transportation for just the mornings. I sent them off to school on the bus and stayed home with Shalva.

I kept her home with me for another week after she was discharged from the hospital to give her time to recuperate and get back to herself. Her teacher and class continued calling every day, which made Shalva feel so good and special.

The last day that I kept Shalva home from school, I told her she was going to school tomorrow. She was so excited and couldn't wait to see all her friends and teachers and be able to learn and have fun in school. I put her to bed early so she should be well rested, and all refreshed going back to school. She fell asleep so excitedly.

CHAPTER: 33

In the morning, she jumped out of bed, saying, "Yay, I'm going to school today!" I bathed her and let her choose her clothing. I made her lunch and packed up her snack. I sent my older children off to school, and then she just couldn't wait to go to school.

She didn't want to waste a second, and she ran to get me her coat and my baby's coat. I bundled them up, put him in the car seat, buckled her into her booster, and I started driving. The whole car ride, she was talking about her friends and school that she missed and how she couldn't wait to go back to school.

As I started parking, reality must have kicked in, and she told me, "Mommy, let's go home." I said, "You were so excited to see your teachers and friends. What's going on?" She said she wanted to stay with me and the baby. I validated her feelings and told her I understood that she wanted to be with us, and we will miss her so much! I told her she's going to have so much fun in school and if there's any problem or her booboos start to hurt, I will tell her teacher to call me. That was very reassuring to her. I took her into her class, gave her hugs and kisses and told the teacher if at any point Shalva looked uncomfortable or in pain or complained, she should call me right away. She said of course, and she gave Shalva a big, warm welcome as I left.

Shalva had a great day back in school. She came home all excited, telling me what she did and who she played with. She said she missed her friends for so long and was happy to be back with them. Every day, when I pick my children up from school, I ask them about their day. This time, they said, before we talk about our day, we want to hear all about Shalva's day back at school. Shalva felt like a star. She told them, and they were all so happy to see her back at school happily.

For the next couple of weeks, I kept a close eye on Shalva. She was acting, playing, and doing everything she should be, without any restrictions. We all went about our day to day lives as usual, while continuing to daven for her.

There's a special mitzvah for a woman to do hafrashas challah (separate some of the dough from the batter, which some people burn and others double wrap and throw out after reciting a blessing on it). So, I decided to try to get forty women every week who are baking challah for Shabbos, to have Shalva in mind as a zchus for a Refuah Shelaima! During the first few months, Baruch Hashem, we were successful with getting forty women every week, and sometimes even more than that. To this day, I still continue to try to get women to bake Challah. Although I don't always reach forty women, every blessing is a zchus and is so powerful. That's what keeps me motivated to continue trying. Every bracha is a zchus, and that is so precious!

The weeks flew by, and it was time for our follow up in the clinic with the whole team of doctors. When we got to the hospital, Shalva first went for blood work. Then we waited until it was our turn to be called on. Not long after, we got called into a room. An OT (Occupational therapist) and PT (Physical therapist) came to evaluate her. I asked them if there was anything natural I could do, and they showed me how to massage her stomach for lymphatic drainage. For another exercise, they drew a diagram and told me I could do it with her once or twice a day. They also recommended that we try some sort of body brace. They measured her and said after it's approved through insurance. It takes some time, and by the time we have to come for our next visit, it should be ready.

The IR came in and asked us many questions. She said at this time, they don't want to proceed with any procedure, though in the future, there are different options. She went through them all with us, explained it to us briefly and said, for now, we will hold off.

I checked the time and knew I wouldn't be home on time for my children. I quickly made some phone calls to arrange for my children to be picked up from school and watched until I got home.

Afterwards, we met with another top doctor, and she brought up the medication again. I told her we were still happy with her off of the medication. Then she said they were still waiting for the lab work to come back regarding the other medication to see if Shalva had that exact cell mutation. If she would, they highly recommend her to go on it.

It was a long, tiring, and draining day. As soon as the appointment was over, we headed straight back home. It was exhausting and tiring. I fed the kids dinner, bathed them, and did the massaging exercise with Shalva. Baruch Hashem, it didn't bother her, which made it easy for me to do.

I then decided to try some natural ways of treating her. I did some of my own personal research and started massaging her stomach with coconut oil every day. Coconut oil is an anti-inflammatory. I did this for a couple of months. Then I started to give her raw garlic cut into tiny pieces to swallow, and I gave her a tablespoon of manuka honey every day. Baruch Hashem, the inflammation seemed to have gone down, and she's been doing well.

I added lemon, ginger, and celery into her diet as there are plenty of natural benefits, and I also gave her probiotics and multivitamins every day.

I was never really into natural remedies, but once I saw that everything medical is trial and error with so many risks of side effects at my last whole experience in the hospital, it opened up my mind to a whole new avenue.

I know the doctors say there is no cure, and I know Hashem can have a cure for everything. I'd be open minded to different ways and open different doors that Hashem has access to cure Shalva in a seemingly natural way.

Everything in life is a miracle, the fact that we wake up every morning, open our eyes, and are able to see and breathe and talk and walk and do whatever we can is all 100% a miracle. Even though it seems so natural, and we don't think of it that way. If for one split second, Hashem decided someone's organ should stop working, it would stop immediately. We tend to take all these things for granted. We think of a miracle as something that happens once in a blue moon and something huge that we wouldn't be able to comprehend. It's our choice if we want to see G-D in our lives. He is with us every second and at every step of the way. Everything is a miracle!

We're not supposed to ask Hashem to do a miracle for us. We have the power to daven and ask for anything we need. We have to do our Hishtadlus, and Hashem can do the rest. So if we do our Hishtadlus and open the gate, Hashem can shower us with blessings.

I decided to be open to some natural ways, and maybe that's the door I have to open for Hashem to be able to give Shalva her cure.

This had been going on for months, and Baruch Hashem Shalva was doing really well. There was some time that I slacked off, and I noticed it got a little inflamed. I showed it to the doctor, and she went on Keflex. I gave Shalva Epsom salt baths and then massaged her with coconut oil and Baruch Hashem it looked and felt much better. We started seeing improvements right away. I continued on with this for a couple of weeks and she loved it and was doing really well.

After some time, we had some holidays, and during those times, I slacked off with the Epsom salt bath and coconut oil massage.

I then tried rubbing castor oil on her. For some reason, it was more ticklish for her. So, as I rub it on her, she's giggling. I switched off some days with castor oil and some days with coconut oil. We still continue with trying to have woman bake Challah as a zchus for her, and we still daven for her and say Tehillim for her every day! We have some women who took upon extra modesty as a zchus for her. Every Tefillah, every good deed is a massive zchus, and I really believe that's what's helping Shalva!

Up until now we would go for follow ups once every three months, now that she is doing well Chasdei Hashem, they said unless there's an emergency or anything spikes up, we have to come in once every six months for a follow up.

Baruch Hashem, she is in kindergarten now. We got her into a great school for Primary next year, and she is really blossoming and growing beautifully.

At this point Baruch Hashem Shalva is a perfect, beautiful, and healthy child. Every fear that the doctors placed upon us has completely vanished. Whenever I see my precious daughter, I keep on going back in time and reminding myself how fast the doctors were trying to persuade us to abort such a perfectly healthy child.

We have seen and heard of stories that doctors have tried to convince parents to abort their babies, and Baruch Hashem, these parents stayed strong to their will and beliefs. They decided against the doctors to keep their pregnancies alive, and the babies came out beautifully healthy.

Unfortunately, there are countless amounts of mothers aborting their children due to concerns and worries, or even pressure from doctors or others.

It's unfortunate that some people really are not knowledgeable and don't know. Had they taken some time to do some more research and followed step by step from the beginning of conception until the baby's first breaths, they would have seen that the process is beyond beautiful, perfect, and miraculous. It's obvious that there must be a G-D behind this fetus.

Without having faith or knowledge that G-D is the one that placed the fetus in the mother's womb, and that G-D will take care of and provide for the child's their entire life. It's easier to come to the conclusion that abortion is the only option. It's the lack of knowledge, pressure, fears, anxiety, and worries that cause some to make these harsh irrational life altering decisions.

And from this, we can all see the Almighty G-D when we see every single detail fall into perfect place. Just like when the baby is conceived until the baby's first breath, you see G-D in every step of the miraculous journey. The very same G-D that created the baby to perfection. If you will give the baby a chance, G-D will continue to take care of this baby to perfection. The question may come up, what if a baby is unhealthy or has a severe illness or disability, which the doctor may be right about or not? That same G-D that molded this fetus according to what G-D perceived as perfection to this specific soul, who are we to question the Creator of all creations? If this is G-D's will, He will give the mother and the child, and anyone involved in the child's life all the means and resources available to perfection. Anyone involved with this child is all designed and orchestrated by G-D. There's no coincidence and no mistake.

This knowledge alone will give strength and certainty that G-D will sustain the baby for its entire life with whatever package the baby is born with. The way it is born has a reason and purpose, which we may never come to understand. Though the soul is born in the type of body and any package it comes along with based on the mission this soul has to accomplish in this world!

CHAPTER: 34

After everything we have just mentioned, there are those who claim that there is no G-D and others who doubt and question G-D's existence.

For some, the miracle of a baby is not enough for them as proof of the existence of G-D. If there is no G-D anyway, let me abort the baby and take the chance to avoid any future sufferings and struggles on our end. To this, we will respond the following.

I can't remember where I heard this from. It says in the Torah that in order for an animal to be kosher, it has to have two signs. 1: It must have completely split Hooves 2: It needs to chew its cud. The verse in Leviticus 11:1-8 says: G-D spoke to Moses and Aaron saying to them. Speak to the Children of Israel saying. These are the creatures that you may eat from among all the land animals. Any animal that has a split hoof, which is completely separated into double hooves, and that chews the cud etc. such you may eat. The Torah continues by saying, the pig's hoof is split, and its hoof is completely separated. It does not chew the cud. It is unclean for you. You shall not eat of their flesh or touch their carcasses; they are unclean for you. In Talmud Bavli Tractate Chulin 59a it quotes this verse and tells us that if there's a man who's walking down the street and finds an animal whose mouth is seriously damaged, he's unable to determine whether the animal is kosher or not, as he can't see if the animal chews its cud. He should check if the animal has completely split Hooves. If the man finds that the animal has split hooves, he can then use the animal as long as he knows with certainty that it is not a pig. (For example, he can look at the tale, and he would be able to know it's not a pig). This is because, according to the Torah, the pig is the only animal in the world that has completely split hooves but does not chew its cud.

This means that every animal in the world that does have split hooves is guaranteed that they also chew their cud, besides the pigs. The pig is the only animal that has split hooves and does not chew its cud. To this very day, we have never encountered any animal that has completely split hooves but does not chew its cud.

Let's digest this for a moment. We received the Torah at Mount Sinai over 3,300 years ago. How is it possible that someone other than the Creator of all the species could've written something like this? That means you would have to know that 8.7 million species of living creatures were in existence without any technology, and with lots of land that was not inhabited by man. We also know that there are many billions of animals that are alive. Thousands and thousands of species whose existence at that time were unknown to man. If a man had written this book, he would not have put his foot in his mouth by claiming this just to be easily contradicted. If a man had wanted to forge the Torah, he would not have exposed himself in such a manner.

To claim that there is only one animal in existence that has split Hooves and does not chew its cud, is a very strong statement. One must know the internal anatomy of about 8.7 million species. The only one who can possibly write such a statement is the Creator Himself.

Let's talk about the moon. I've heard this from my teacher, Rabbi Yosef Mizrachi, he should be healthy and strong. The Hebrew calendar is very precise and exact. For example, we must fast on Yom Kippur, and we are well aware that Hashem is strict with His commandments. So, we cannot mess up the calendar days, as we may not mistakenly fast on the wrong day and eat on Yom Kippur. Let's go back in time before calendars were invented. When we saw the new moon, we would know it is the first day of the Jewish month. The new moon is the period of time at the beginning of the month when the moon is not visible through the naked eye. The process goes as follows; There was a Sanhedrin (a great Jewish court) where two witnesses would show up to court and they would testify that they saw the new moon. The witnesses would be

229

interrogated with many questions until the Sanhedrin would feel confident enough to declare a new month.

In Talmud Bavli Tractate Rosh Hashanah, page 25a, there's a story brought down. It was a really cloudy day, and two witnesses came to testify about the renewal of the moon in the Sanhedrin in front of Raban Gamliel (The head of the Sanhedrin). The witnesses said that they saw the renewal of the new moon. Raban Gamliel responded to the witnesses that it cannot be true. You have not seen the new moon. The witnesses responded back asking; is it possible that we are both wrong? Raban Gamliel responded back and said yes. We have a tradition that goes from generation to generation all the way back to Moshe Rabeinu (Moses), who received it from G-D that the renewal of the moon cannot ever be less than 29½ days and ⅔ of an hour and 73 parts of a minute. Get your thinking caps on for a moment as we calculate. 29 days and ½ day (12 hours) ⅔ of an hour (40 minutes) 73 parts of a minute (0.822 seconds) adds up to 29.530590 days per month. That's the calculation of the Torah. Raban Gamliel told them that he's been keeping track of time, and you came a bit too early.

Let's look at the scientific world to see what they have to say about the minimum cycle of the moon. In the Earth's moon system cycle NASA published the calculations to be 29.530590.

NASA works with satellites and with many employees on a twenty-billion-dollar budget. They came to the exact same calculation as the Torah.

As we said a bit earlier, the Torah was given over 3,300 years ago, before any technology, satellites, or mega computers existed, and there was no way to measure these calculations. This is a number with six digits after the decimal point. How were they able to make such a brilliant calculation without any outside resources? We see the number is exact to the theory as the scientists have proven. There is no coincidence, there must be the Creator who knows His exact calculations of His creation. These two proofs that we just mentioned above are not even a drip in the ocean of what our sages of blessed memory have taught us.

Let's think logically for a moment. If I were to tell you that this beautiful car was created by itself through a random explosion, you'd probably laugh me off and tell me to seek medical attention. The rule in life is, as we clearly see, when there is a creation, there must be a creator. Now, let's sit back and look at the world and how every part of nature is beyond perfect. And now, to claim that all the beautiful creations just happened with a bang does not seem logical or clever. If there needs to be a creator for a car or a light bulb, how much more so for an entire universe and everything and everyone in it?

After all the evidence that we just discussed and with 100% certainty, we know that there is One G-D, the Creator of the world. Before making such a life altering decision of terminating a pregnancy, which is a beautiful creation of G-D, think all this through and let it process.

Some may wonder, if I can chop down a tree that is G-D's creation, why can't I abort a baby that's G-D's creation?

Every creation that G-D created was a gift that G-D gave to us. So that's why we are able to take another creation and destroy it if it's for our benefit. For example, to chop down a tree to build a house, to kill an animal in a humane fashion in order to eat it so we can have proper nutrients, health, and energy so we can serve G-D.

One may ask, why can't I abort the baby if it's assumed to be for the mother's benefit? Just like we said, you can chop down a tree for your benefit to build a house. The answer to that is simple. You are using the actual tree for your benefit after the tree has been chopped. In the case of an abortion, you do not benefit in any way from the actual fetus after the abortion. It seems that the fetus was created without any purpose, so it must be that this creation's purpose is to be born and let G-D figure out the rest.

As we mentioned, all of G-D's creations have to be able to benefit mankind. Otherwise, why would G-D have created it? It must be that this fetus, soon to be baby, has to be of benefit to the world and be able to help society. As for the mother who is unable to see the benefit at the present moment, patience is a great attribute.

By doing an abortion, not only are you taking the life of a fetus, but you're actually taking lives away for generations to come as well. There are women who are not capable of raising a child. That's not a good enough reason not to give the baby a chance for life.

There are those who are truly scared that they won't be able to manage. Whether it's financially, mentally, or physically. There are numerous organizations and resources available to help. However, termination should be used in extreme circumstances with the guidance of a spiritual leader, a Rabbi, and a medical doctor when the mother's life is endangered by the pregnancy.

Imagine your parents decided to terminate their pregnancy when you were the fetus. You wouldn't have a chance in life to make anything out of yourself.

The fact that you exist shows that there is a purpose, and the fact that a baby was conceived, shows that there's a purpose to that as well.

Many people have asked us over the years through our journey, how are you guys coping, functioning, and managing, and going about your day-to-day life while providing for the family, and running a full-time household? It sounds unbearable. It's not something people would just go around saying life's beautiful, great and dandy. The honest truth is it's really hard and scary. At times, it took a tremendous toll on our relationship as a couple. We came to the understanding that if we don't stay strong and hold down the fort, our relationship and family will fall apart. Which we have seen countless times, when couples go through challenging situations. At times, there's an enormous amount of stress, and the marriage kind of just disintegrates as they don't have the whereabouts and foundation to hold up the building, instead of utilizing and using these challenges as cement for a foundation.

It's a choice and an opportunity one has when faced with difficulties and challenges to strengthen the foundation of their relationship or let the challenge get the better of them and let the relationship dwindle. Life will only get better when there's a team with unity.

Have you ever noticed when work is being done on the roads and traffic is backed up for miles? You see a handful of guys working in a tiny hole. Those guys are there trying to diagnose and fix a problem. Imagine some workers didn't show up to work one day, and there was only one man working solely to fix this on his own. It would be a nightmare. He may be able to fix the issue, though it'll take a lot more energy, toiling, and time. And in the end, he may have to wait for help to come as somethings are at least a two-man job. His life would've been a lot easier, smoother, and more relaxed had the team of workers shown up. When you don't work as a team, it's not just you that is affected, the entire world around you gets affected as well. As in this case, the traffic jam lasted way longer than it should have. People wouldn't be late to school, work, and appointments had the team showed up and worked in unity.

We made the choice to tackle what came our way as a team ready to play the Super Bowl, and losing was not an option. We also decided to make all our children a part of our team. We had a great big team, and when the baby was born, we added a player, he became the cutest mascot. A team will only be successful with a great coach. And for that, we have Hashem.

We explained to all the players that Hashem was going to guide us, and we would work really hard to listen to all the instructions and rules as best as we possibly could.

What are the rules? For that, we have to turn to the Torah and our sages of blessed memory. The definition of the Hebrew word Torah (Bible) means instructions. The Torah is a handbook of how to live our lives with the exact instructions on how to go about everything. By following the Torah, we will be able to tackle all the challenges and live a blessed life of happiness, faith, love, and fear of Hashem. Even during hard times, we are able to find the beauty in it all, as we know Hashem orchestrates everything perfectly and for a purpose.

One of the main rules that we learn is to always have the concept; that all that G-D does is perfect and for the best! As a family, we all constantly practice, preach, and live this way! As confusing as it may have been for us, we stuck with our faith and morals. This gave us great comfort, security, and courage to move forward through life during these challenging times.

I heard an incredible insight from Rav Shimon Schwab explaining and putting life into perspective through the following: Why do we dip Maror (Bitter Herbs) into Charoses (a sweet dip made with fruits, nuts, wine, spices and honey...) at the Pesach (Passover) seder? We do this to relive and commemorate what our ancestors went through while we were slaves to Paroah (Pharaoh) in Mitzrayim (Egypt). We eat the bitter herbs as a reminder that those times were really bitter. By eating the maror, we are teaching, reliving and re-experiencing the pain and suffering that our ancestors experienced during that time frame. We eat the Charoses to commemorate the back breaking labor of making cement for the pyramids that our ancestors built. As Charoses has the appearance of cement.

The question is as follows, why is Charoses sweet? As the times were so bitter, could we not have made the appearance look like cement but not be so tasty, sweet, and delicious? Couldn't we make it more sour and bitter to really feel the pain and suffering that they went through in Mitzrayim? Why is it so sweet? The answer to this is astonishing; during the Pesach Seder, we are trying to teach and relive the experience that our ancestors went through. As they were going through their darkness and bitter times, the righteous men of that generation were constantly saying that everything that G-D does is for the best. They saw this cement with sweetness as they knew it was ultimately coming from G-D, and everything that G-D does is for our benefit. It's for the best, and it's really sweet in the deeper picture, even though, at face value, it may seem otherwise.

We decided to try our best to live by this motto that everything Hashem does is for the best. Even through challenges and darkness, there is sweetness, and it's there to help us grow. We are aware it was not an easy journey for anyone involved in building the Empire State Building to get it to reach its height. Yet they did it with motivation as they saw the finished product before they even started. We know that when someone goes through any difficulty or challenge in life, they are not in it alone. G-D is with them and going through the actual pain together so to speak. G-D is the creator who knows what the finished product looks like before the journey even begins. We have to put all our faith and belief in Hashem that the finished product is beautiful and that there will be light at the end of the tunnel. We just have to keep strong, be patient and hold on tight to Hashem.

Letting go and letting G-D take full control can be challenging in itself. The way we go about our tough, challenging hardships is, we try to look back at our personal lives and we reflect on all the challenging moments we were faced with up until this very point. We would then openly discuss with each other how everything works out with time. When it felt that the world was coming to an end, it was one door closing while a bigger and better door was opening. We just have to be patient while we are faced with hardships. It would be a good idea to keep a scoreboard of every challenge you are faced with, how you felt going through the challenge, and the growth and outcome when the challenge passed.

There are many times that people are fired or laid off from their jobs, and they feel resentment and frustration. They even may come to question G-D. Does He not know I need to put food on the table for my children? A few days or weeks pass he ends up with a much better paying job, and he feels sad that he spoke and felt the way he did towards himself, and G-D. Hashem was actually helping and setting him up by opening up a new door. Had he not been fired or laid off, he would not have had this greater opportunity. Now, he has so much gratitude and love towards G-D. Imagine how much greater he would feel about himself, and more gratitude he would have towards G-D had he responded to this situation positively from the beginning.

We learned a lot throughout our journey. The biggest lesson we learned is emunah (faith) and bitachon (trust). From time and time again, how all the pieces are put together makes you open your eyes and realize that the strings are being pulled from somewhere. Just as we sit back and enjoy a bus ride or relax on a boat or a plane, we trust the driver and pilot that they will get you to your destination safely. So, too, in life there is a pilot that is Hashem, so let's sit back and enjoy the ride.

Looking back at the very first moment that we saw Shalva and the questions that we asked, the truth is we wouldn't have wanted it in any other way. Shalva is four years old, and Baruch Hashem is beyond perfect. Our family, along with Shalva, had to go through this continuous journey, and only Hashem knows why. Being the parents of Shalva is an honor and privilege that Hashem bestowed upon us for this job! She is our treasure!

Anyone who doesn't know her and sees her would not think she has any booboo. She's a precious cute girl and looks perfectly beautiful and normal. She is a bright girl with a real happy and positive disposition. She's with it and has the cutest personality! We are so grateful to Hashem for her. We feel so blessed to be her parents! I don't know why she had to be born with this and why she had to go through all that she's been through, though we feel very blessed, honored and privileged to be her parents! We feel like we won the lottery by having her! She is the most perfect child, a real blessing and a true miracle! She made us stronger and taught us to see the world through a different lens and appreciate everything without taking small things for granted! Thank you,

Hashem, for gifting us with Shalva and may she continue to blossom and grow and be fully cured! May she be a real source of light to the world, and may she be a great role model to all those around her. She should always be a walking, talking Kiddush Hashem! (Sanctifying Hashem)

THE END!

GLOSSARY

- Achdus: Unity
- Baruch Hashem: Blessed is G-D
- Bentch(ed): Blessings said at the conclusion of a meal
- Bikur Cholim: Visiting the sick
- Bikur Cholim Room: Kosher pantry
- Bitachon: Trust
- Bris: A ceremony that takes place on the eighth day after the birth of a baby boy when he gets circumcised
- Bubby: Grandma
- Candle lighting: A customary tradition to light candles to honor and welcome in Shabbos Chag: Holiday
- Charoses: A sweet dip made with fruits, nuts, wine, spices, honey...
- Chasdei Hashem: With the kindness of G-D
- Chein: Grace
- Chesed: Giving of yourself with love and compassion, an act of kindness
- Chevra Kaddisha: An organization of people that prepare the deceased for a proper burial with in accordance to jewish law
- Chizuk: Inspiration
- Daf Yomi: Learning a page of Gemara every day
- Daven(ing): Pray(ing)
- Dvar Torah: A small speech regarding a subject in the Torah
- Emunah: Faith/Belief
- Gam Zu LTova: This too is for the best
- Gemara: Talmud
- Hakaros Hatov: Gratitude
- Halacha: Jewish law
- Hatzalah: Jewish volunteer medical service

- Har Sinai: Mount Sinai, the mountain where the Jewish people received the Torah

- Hashem: G-D

- Hashgacha Pratis: Divine Providence

- Hishtadlus: Personal efforts

- Hodu L'Hashem Ki Tov Ki Lolom Chasdo: Thank G-D for His goodness, because His grace is forever

- Hoshana Rabbah: It's a Jewish festival during Sukkos, it's a holy day where the judgements of Rosh

- Hashanah and Yom Kippur are ratified

- Kaddish: It's a mourners prayer about faith and giving praise to the almighty

- Kibud Av: Honoring your father

- Kiddush: Before the start of a meal on Shabbos, holidays and other special occasions that we recite a blessing over wine

- Kiddush Hashem: Sanctifying Hashem's name through a

religious or moral act, that causes others to respect Hashem Maror: Bitter Herbs

- Matzav: Situation

- Mazel Tov: Congratulations

- Menucha: Peace, tranquility

- Minyan: The quorum of 10 men gathered together to pray

- Mitzrayim: Egypt

- Mitzvos: Commandments

- Mi K'amcha Yisrael: Who is like the Jewish nation

- Motzei Shabbos: Saturday night

- Muktzah: Items that are prohibited from using on Shabbos and on holidays

- Neshama: Soul

- Paroah: Pharoah

- Pekelach: Party bags filled with some nosh, candies

- Pesach: Passover, one of the three major jewish holidays celebrating the exodus of Egypt

- Purim: A Jewish festival, holiday

- » Rabbi: A Jewish scholar, spiritual leader
- » Refuah Shelaima: A complete and speedy recovery
- » Rofeh: A Healer, doctor
- » Sanhedrin: A great Jewish court
- » Schmoozing: Chatting
- » Seudah: Meal
- » Sefarim: Biblical books
- » Shabbos: Sabbath, Shabbat, the seventh day of the week, a holy day that we focus on a spiritual connection with G-D
- » Shavuos: Shavuot, one of the three major jewish holidays, we celebrate the giving of the Torah at Mount Sinai
- » Shachris: Morning prayers
- » Shaliach: Messenger
- » Shema: A prayer said before one goes to sleep at night
- » Shiurim: Lectures
- » Shul: Synagogue
- » Simcha: Joy, happiness. A celebration on a happy, special occasion
- » Simchas Torah: A very joyous day that we celebrate the conclusion and restart the annual cycle of reading the Torah, with singing and dancing with the Torah.
- » Sukkah: A temporary hut, shelter that we eat and lodge in during Sukkos
- » Sukkos: It's one of the three major holidays, it's a joyous festival
- » Teffilah, Teffilos: Prayers
- » Teffilin: Phylacteries
- » Tehillim: A book of Psalms
- » Todah Hashem: Thank you G-D
- » Torah: Bible
- » Tov L'hodos L'Hashem: It's Good to give Thanks To G-D
- » Tzedakah: Charity
- » Tzedaka Tatzil Mimaves: Charity saves from death
- » Yartzeit: The anniversary of the death of a person
- » Yom Tov: Holiday
- » Zechus, Zchus: Merit
- » Zemiros: Zemirot, Songs